DOVER-FOYLE HAND

BASKET.

F. J. CHRISTOPHER

Edited by

MARJORIE O'SHAUGHNESSY

DOVER PUBLICATIONS, INC. NEW YORK

This Dover edition, first published in 1952, is an unabridged and slightly revised republication of the work originally published in 1951. This reprint is published by special arrangement with W. & G. Foyle, Ltd., publishers of the original edition.

Standard Book Number: 486-20677-7
Library of Congress Catalog Card Number: 53-9932

Manufactured in the United States of America
Dover Publications, Inc.
180 Varick Street
New York, N.Y. 10014

CONTENTS

CONTENTS—*cont.*

properties — making a basket — working sequence — finishing. **Basket:** Lucite base. **A Napkin Ring:** Useful article — commencing — working — practise.

CONTENTS—*cont.*

PREFACE

BASKETRY, that is, the making of useful and often beautiful containers from natural materials, is one of the oldest crafts known to man. The reason is not far to seek, for there is no country in the world where there is not some kind of plant which can be used for twisting into baskets. In temperate zones such as Europe, use was made and still is, of willow canes, rushes and so on, while in the hotter countries of the Equatorial belt, cane, bamboo and palm leaves could all be pressed into service.

Primitive man had few tools but he was able to make all kinds of things simply by twisting together the materials he found nearest to his hand. As time went on, he improved on his basketwork huts and boats and found other materials for them, but he went on using woven materials for baskets and other containers, devoting his increasing skill to improving and beautifying them.

Many of the baskets made in the earliest times were, of course, intended for everyday use and naturally they wore out. Enough fragments have survived, however, for us to be able to realise how widespread the craft was, and what man's earliest efforts looked like.

Coiled basketry, which is one of the earliest forms of basketry known, has been found in many parts of the world and there are primitive tribes in Africa and South America which still produce beautiful examples of this form of the craft. Intricate and very lovely patterns are worked into these baskets, many of them being symbolical designs which have been handed down from mother to daughter, for generations.

F.J.C.

CHAPTER I

Introduction — variety of materials — brief history of the craft — preparation and treatment — sizes — fascination of basketry. **Materials:** Quality — Reed — Willow — Hong Kong grass — Raffia — Rushes — Coiled basketry — Raffia, thick string, rope; descriptions and uses — other materials — Plastics. **Tools and Equipment:** Few and simple — knife, scissors, pliers — improvised equipment — boards. **Care of Tools, Material and Equipment:** Storing and cleaning — storing materials — a cool place needed — wooden bases — wetting. **Technical Terms:** Professional terms — amateur knowledge — simple explanation of terms.

As I have already mentioned geography has played a great part in determining the type of basket made by the inhabitants of particular parts of the earth. In England, for instance, up to quite recent times, when it became possible to import reed, the majority of baskets were made from willow, probably because the type of willow grown in Northern Europe is excellent for the purpose. In Norway and Sweden baskets are made from split wood, and this branch of the craft is still found in various parts of England, a good example being the sturdy Royal Sussex trug, beloved of gardeners. This localising of the craft is found all over the world, where each country and almost every district had or still has its own peculiar type of basket—a basket which is often used only in this one locality.

When we turn to the Far East, we find a completely different form of basketry for here the natural materials available are cane, bamboo and various types of palm leaves. Both the Chinese and Japanese people are recognized as experts in the making of baskets and furniture from bamboo. The basketry work of the North American Indians has, of course, become world-famous.

Palm leaf basketry is a branch of the craft which flourishes in the East Indies. Here, several varieties of palm leaf are used, all of them, however, having one characteristic in common—that of being capable of being split into pieces of any width.

Nowadays a vast amount of basketry is carried out with reed, of which I shall have more to say later.

This brief sketch will, I hope, serve to show how universal and important the craft of basketry is. Those of us who follow it, in however amateur a fashion, are therefore helping to carry on a tradition which is as old as man himself. The more one learns about the craft, the more interesting it becomes. Never be content merely to read about it. Get some reed and make a basket for yourself. An ounce of practise is worth a ton of theory in basketry, as in all other crafts. Once you have experienced the fascination of making a basket, you will want to go on and on, and you will find that there is always something new to learn.

MATERIALS

A consideration of the history of basketry leads us naturally to the question of what materials are available to the worker of today. By far the most easily obtained and simplest to use, is reed. Here a word of warning is necessary. Never be tempted to buy inferior reed, because it is a few cents cheaper. Poor reed is difficult to work with and the finished article is seldom worth the time and trouble you have spent on it.

'Pulp' cane as it is often called, is a rather misleading term for the type of reed used for making baskets, for in actual fact it is very hard and not in the least pulpy, as its name might imply. A better term is reed, or 'centre' cane, for that is what the cane actually is.

Rattan or cane palms are found growing wild in tropical countries, the best types being found in the Dutch East Indies. They are climbing plants which grow to a great length, sometimes as much as 600 feet. The diameter of the stem seldom gets much larger than one inch. At first the plants are erect, but when they get to be several feet long, they need some kind of support. They therefore put out long feelers with hooked thorns which cling to the trees and bushes around. The plant has few leaves and these grow only at the end of the stem. The centre spine of the leaves projects for a distance of about 18 in. beyond the end of the leaf and as the stem, underside of the leaf and the projecting piece are all protected by the hooked thorns, it is not an easy matter to gather the cane. The natives who do the work cut the branches with an axe and then leave them to hang in the sun, so that the outer covering will shrivel up and so become easier to remove. When this has been done, the reeds are cut into convenient lengths, tied into bundles and shipped to the ports where they are graded into sizes ready for export to the factories which turn them into the familiar pulp cane or reed which we buy for our basketwork.

Round reeds are the ones commonly used in basketry. These are numbered according to size, which is computed in millimetres. The ones most used are Nos. 2 and 3 for weaving, No. 4 for the spokes or stakes and No. 8 for handles. The actual sizes are:

No.	Millimetres	No.	Millimetres
0	$1\frac{1}{4}$ (1/64″)	6	$4\frac{1}{4}$
1	$1\frac{1}{2}$ (1/32″)	7	5
2	2 (1/16″)	8	6
3	$2\frac{1}{4}$ (3/32″)	9	7
4	$2\frac{3}{4}$ (7/64″)	10	8
5	$3\frac{1}{4}$ (1/8″)	11	9

Half-sizes are only used commercially and are sold in bulk. Any of the sizes enumerated above may be bought by the pound, prices ranging downward from about $1.50 a pound. The differences in sizes are not so great that they may not be used interchangeably. If you are working from instructions that call for No. 2 reed, for example, it will not alter the results appreciably if you use No. 3.

Of flat reeds, three widths are customarily used in basketry: $\frac{1}{4}$″ $\frac{3}{8}$″ and $\frac{1}{2}$″.

Flat oval reed, which is flat on one side and oval on the other, is used mostly for chair seats. The popular widths for this purpose are $5/16$″, $7/16$″ and $\frac{3}{8}$″. Flat and flat oval reeds are currently sold at slightly over a dollar a pound.

Willow, though a traditional material for basket construction is more difficult to work with than reed, and for this reason should not be used by the beginner. When you have had some experience of using reed and have mastered the various 'strokes,' you will be able to tackle the making of baskets with willow, but not before.

Hong Kong grass, an attractive material, can be used for weaving baskets, stool tops and chair seats. In its natural state, the grass is a coarse grass or sedge. It is twisted to form a continuous length, and can be obtained in both a natural shade and in colours.

When we come to coiled basketry, we find that the list of possible materials is growing. Raffia is used for the actual sewing of the coils but as the latter are completely hidden during the working, other materials besides reed can be used. These include the raffia itself, used in a bundle of strands varying in number according to the thickness of the coil you require. Thick string or rope can be used when a really thick coil is needed and are to be preferred to reed, since if reed in the same thickness were to be used, you would find it extremely difficult to work.

Raffia comes from the dried leaves of a species of palm found chiefly in Madagascar. The leaves have to be cut before they start to uncurl. The tough underpart is stripped away and, when dry, can be split from end to end. The strips vary in width and can be split again quite easily if you need a narrower piece.

Raffia in a variety of colours, as well as in its natural colour, can be bought in craft shops.

Raffia, like reed, should be of as good a quality as you can get. Cheap raffia will split and fray and probably prove to be dearer in the long run.

In addition to the actual reed, willow or raffia, you will need several other materials. Of these, wood is the most important. A great many basketwork articles, such as trays, teapot stands and so on, are made on a wood base. The best woods to use are oak and birch. The latter is a little cheaper than the former. Wooden bases with the holes for the reed already drilled can be bought for baskets and trays in many sizes and shapes, coasters and other articles.

Any plywood which will not warp can be used, and if it is not of very good quality, it can be stained and varnished or enamelled.

Many people like to use glass in trays and teapot stands, but though it may be an asset in the latter case, I feel that a glass base in a tray makes the article rather heavy. Plastics could be used, but it is as well when making use of plastic materials in this way, to make sure that the material is really heat-resistant.

During the last few years, plastic materials of all kinds have come on to the market in increasing numbers. Plastic wire can be used in much the same way as reed, for weaving small articles. It looks best when used in conjunction with other plastic materials. Wood and plastic wire, or plastic material and reed (which, after all, is a kind of wood) do not, in my opinion, really harmonise very well, mainly I think, because one is a natural and the other a synthetic product.

TOOLS AND EQUIPMENT

The tools required for basketry are few in number but they must be of good quality. Some are essential, others are useful, but you can manage without them if you have to. You must have a really sharp knife for you will need it for cutting off the ends and shaving them when necessary.

A pair of round-nosed pliers is another essential tool. They are needed for squeezing the reed when you want to bend it at an acute angle, as you will when working borders. If the reed is not well-squeezed before it is bent, it will crack and split, instead of bending around smoothly. You may also want a pair of flat-nosed pliers.

Next comes an awl, which is used for making the spaces in the weaving when you wish to put in new stakes for a handle, and so on. Probably you will also wish to invest in a reed cutter and a diagonal cutter.

All these tools, which are sold singly or in sets, average about two dollars each, except the awl, which costs about a quarter.

British basketmakers use a tool called a rapping iron, which might equally well be called a tapping iron. This resembles a chisel except that it is not sharpened at the end and is used particularly in willow work for tapping

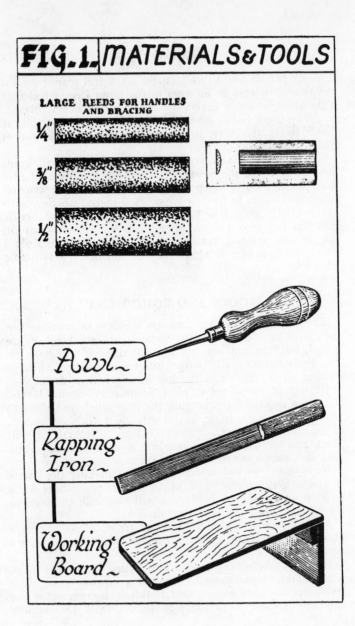

FIG. 1. MATERIALS & TOOLS

LARGE REEDS FOR HANDLES
AND BRACING

¼"

⅜"

½"

Awl

*Rapping
Iron*

*Working
Board*

down the weaving so that it is firm and level. This useful iron is not a regular part of the American basketmaker's equipment and will not be easy to find. If you are not able to buy one, you can use a chisel or any piece of iron like the one in the illustration.

Coiled basketry requires a blunt tapestry needle with a large eye.

If you wish to make a stool or re-cane a chair, you will need one or two special tools but I will mention these when I reach the chapter dealing with these two subjects.

Equipment for basketry is simple and easy to make for yourself. Articles with a wooden base can rest on a bench or table but those with a reed base should be pegged to a work board as soon as the base is completed. Professional workers use a light board or piece of planking, one end of which rests on the floor, while the other rests against the worker's knee. The length of the plank depends upon the individual worker. The basket is pegged at right angles to the board and slopes away from the worker.

The second type of board consists of two pieces of wood, one round about 12" x 8" and the other about 6" x 8", nailed together as shown in Fig. 1. The board rests on a table with the raised end at the back and the basket is pegged to the sloping side. In this case the work slopes towards the person making the basket. With both types of board, care must be taken to see that the basket revolves easily as the work proceeds.

CARE OF TOOLS, MATERIAL AND EQUIPMENT

Good work, as I have said, cannot be done with poor tools and inferior materials. A good deal can be done, however, towards keeping your equipment in the best condition.

Tools should not be allowed to lie about, where they can become rusty. Knives must be kept sharp and clean. A dirty knife or pliers can easily make a mark that you will not be able to remove.

Although reed, willow and rushes have to be used while they are damp, as I shall explain later, they must always be allowed to become thoroughly dry before you put them away. If this is not done, both reed and raffia tend to become discoloured while other materials become mildewed if stored in a damp place. If damp raffia is wound into a bundle, it turns brown as well as holding the water for a surprisingly long time.

You will generally find that the reeds you buy are too long to use as they are. Most reed has been folded once in packing and the loop thus formed is often difficult to remove. If you cut the reed about an inch or so on either side of the bend, you will remove this disadvantage and make your reeds of a workable length. When you wish to put away the reed, bend your bundle in half, tie near the end with a piece of string and either hang on a nail or lay on a rack of some kind.

Never store any natural materials in a dry hot place. Heat will dry out the natural moisture and cause them to shrivel or crack. Reed should be kept covered if you do not wish to use it immediately, so that it will not gather dust. Raffia should be tied into a bundle and stored in a large brown paper bag.

Wooden bases should be bought as required. If you have to store them, see that they are not too near a source of heat or they may warp. It is impossible to make a good article unless the base is perfectly flat.

When you are dampening reed during working, be careful not to let any water fall on to the wooden base, as this may cause a stain which cannot be removed.

Space—considerable work space—is needed for the practice of basketry, and it is a rather messy operation because of the necessity for keeping material damp. It is therefore not a craft that can be pursued in a corner of the living room (while looking at television). It also calls for a patient and careful temperament.

Most kinds of reedwork last a very long time, if they are well made in the first place, but naturally they do not stay clean indefinitely. Reed and willow can be brushed or washed in clear warm water. Soap should not be used as it tends to lodge in the cracks. Raffia work can be washed with soap and water. It should be allowed to dry naturally away from a fire, though if it is left out in the sun, it will become slightly bleached.

Most plastic materials, enamelled bases, etc., can be cleaned quite easily with a damp cloth.

TECHNICAL TERMS

There are not a great many technical terms which it is essential for you to know. Professional basketmakers naturally have their own terms, but it is sufficient for the amateur to know only the most general of them.

The upright reeds which form the foundation upon which the basket is woven are known as stakes or spokes. When it becomes necessary to insert extra stakes by the side of the first ones so that the work will be stronger, these are known as bi-stakes. Many workers prefer this method of giving additional strength as two thinner stakes placed side by side are neater and flatter than one thick one.

When you start to weave the sides of a basket, the stakes or spokes have to be fixed firmly in place. This process of setting up (or as British basketmakers call it, "upsetting") is done by a three-ply coil weave. If the stakes are not fixed in place very securely when the setting up is started, you will never be able to make the basket a good shape, no matter how much trouble you take.

The simplest kind of weaving with reed is, of course, the ordinary over-and-under, in front of one stake and behind the next, with a single piece of reed. In English basketry, this is called randing. When working this type of weaving, you should have an uneven number of stakes, or you will find that when you reach the end of the first row, you will have to go in front of, or behind two stakes next to one another. Should you for any reason find that you must have an even number of stakes, you can get over the difficulty by using two weavers. Work a row of over-and-under with the first reed and when you come to the start of the second row, drop this and weave a row with the second reed. Continue working with alternate reeds in this way until the required amount has been done.

Pairing is the name given to the method of weaving in which you use two reeds at the same time, working one stroke with each reed alternately. Sometimes two or more reeds are used side by side as if they were only one. This method is sometimes called slewing, double over-and-under or twined weaving.

Directions for working several different types of weaving will be found a little further on, when we come to the actual making of basketwork articles. I have tried to include as many varieties as possible, but it must be understood that the different types of working are interchangeable, although naturally some types are more suitable for a particular article than others.

There are various names given to borders but these need not worry you. Borders are used to finish off the weaving as a means of anchoring the stakes and making sure that the weaving will not become loose. They are usually worked with the top parts of the upright stakes, although it is sometimes necessary to use additional reeds when the border is a fairly elaborate one. Base borders are used on articles made on a wooden base, as a means of fixing the stakes in place. The base border is always worked first.

Braided borders make an extremely attractive finish to baskets or trays and there are several varieties, distinguished by the number of reeds used. Braids may be vertical or horizontal according to the taste of the worker and the purpose for which the article is meant to be used. Baskets look well with a vertical braid, while trays are better with a flat braid which makes the tray easier to carry.

Scalloped borders are sometimes used on small articles. They are suitable for table mats and very small baskets, but since they consist simply of upright stakes bent over and pushed down beside a stake a little farther on, they will not stand up to really hard wear.

The 'stroke' is the name given to one complete movement of the weaving reed. It corresponds to the stitch in knitting or sewing.

FIG. 2. | A TEA POT STAND.

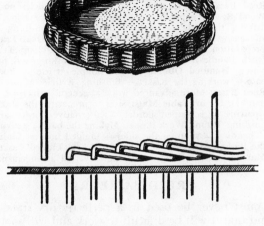

FOOT BORDER

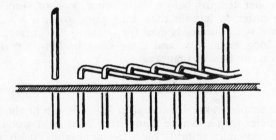

ALTERNATIVE FOOT BORDER

REED BASKETRY

REED must never be used in a perfectly dry state or you will find that it will be difficult to work and will soon crack. There is no need to soak it. Dip it into cold water and let it lie in a sink or bath for a few minutes. I find that when a large number of stakes is required, it is best to cut them into the proper lengths before dampening, as short pieces are much easier to handle than long ones, particularly when they are wet. The reeds used for weaving, of course, should be as long as possible and these must be lightly coiled so that you can handle them easily.

REED ARTICLES ON A WOOD BASE

The teapot stand illustrated in Fig. 2 is one of the smallest articles which can be made from reed on a wood base, and is especially suitable for a beginner, since it gives him quite a lot of practice in handling the material, with very little risk of spoiling it. The directions for making the stand I am giving rather more fully than for the articles you will find further on, since I am assuming that the reader is a complete beginner to the craft.

To make the teapot stand shown in Fig 2, you will need a circular base 6" in diameter and about ½ oz. of No. 2 reed. The base can be finished off in several ways. It can be painted or enamelled but varnish should be avoided as it tends to become sticky when a hot teapot is placed on it. An alternative method is to use a piece of plain glass under which you can put a dainty paper doily or a piece of patterned wallpaper, a poster board on which is painted a design of some kind or a piece of embroidered material. Circles of ordinary glass cut to the size required can usually be obtained quite cheaply from shops selling articles for house decoration. The glass, and whatever is put under it, should be cut so that they fit just inside the holes drilled for the reed, so that the weaving will hold them firmly in place.

If your base is one bought specially for the purpose, the holes will be already drilled. If you make your own base from thin plywood, cut it to size very carefully, and sandpaper each side and all round the edge very thoroughly. Drill holes all around about ⅝" apart and ¼" in from the edge. Sandpaper any little roughnesses that may result. When drilling holes for reed work, remember that they must be just large enough to allow the reed to pass through easily without being forced. If the holes are too small the outside of the reed will be stripped off and the appearance of the finished article will be spoilt because the reed looks rough. If the holes are too large, the reeds will slip about and the work will be sloppy instead of firm.

Count the holes and cut the same number of pieces of No. 2 reed, each 8" long. (Notice that in the case of the teapot stand, it does not matter whether the number of holes is odd or even.) Damp the reed by allowing it to lie in a bowl of water for a few minutes, then shake off the surplus moisture. If you have to put the work aside, or if the reeds become dry as you work as they will if you are working on a hot day or in a hot room, moisten them again.

Push one reed through each hole so that about 3½" projects on the under side. Place the base on the table so that the longer ends of the stakes are pointing away from you and work a foot border as follows: Take one of the shorter ends that will be pointing towards you and bend it gently towards the right, putting it behind the stake immediately to the right of it, in front of the next two and behind the next. Leave the end here, pointing it inwards, and be sure to press it well down on to the wood base. Take the second right hand stake and repeat the movement. A glance at Fig. 2 will show you what your work should look like. Note that in all the diagrams, I have drawn the reeds as if they were worked loosely, so that the method can be seen more clearly. In actual fact, of course, the reeds must be pressed as close together as possible.

Continue in the same way until there are only three stakes which are still standing. You now have to finish off the border so that the join cannot be seen. Ease up the first three stakes carefully and gently with the awl and weave in the upstanding stakes one by one, matching the pattern carefully. Then pull up the border by pulling the upstanding stakes on the other side of the base.

Fig. 2 shows an alternative pattern for a border. It is worked in the same way as the one already described, but each stake goes behind one stake, in front of the next and behind the next, leaving the ends pointing inwards as before. This border is slightly smaller and lighter in appearance than the first one and is suitable for small articles such as coasters.

Note that in making any foot border, the stakes must be long enough to go right behind the last upright stake and project for at least an inch on to the base, or they will be liable to spring out again as you work. The thicker the reed, the longer the stakes need to be.

When the base border is complete, turn the work right side up with the base resting on the table. Place the glass on top with whatever decoration you have chosen placed underneath it. You are now ready to weave the sides. In this case, the method used is that known as three-ply coil weave or triple twist. Practise doing this until you can do it really well, for you will find that it is a very useful method to know and one which is used at the base of many types of basket.

Take three pieces of No. 2 reed and damp them. Place them in the spaces between three consecutive stakes, so that

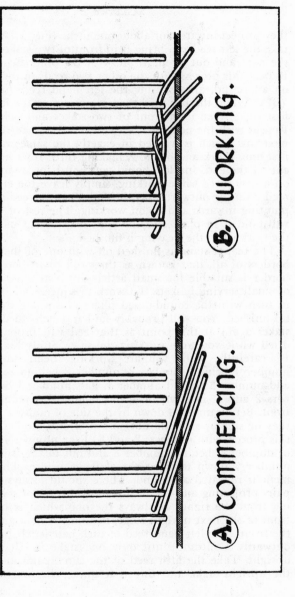

FIG. 3. WORKING THE SIDES.

A. COMMENCING.

B. WORKING.

they project inwards for about one inch. (Fig. 3 (A)). Now take the left reed and bring it in front of two stakes, behind the next and out to the front, over the other two weavers. Repeat this process with the other two reeds in turn and go on all round, always using the left hand reed (see Fig. 3 (B)). When the last used reed comes out to the left of the first stake, take it in front of two stakes and behind one. Repeat with the next two reeds. You are now ready for the next row which is worked in exactly the same way as the first one. Work another row, making three rows in all, and cut off the ends inside. Should you find it necessary to join on a new piece while working, simply leave the end of the reed pointing outwards, lay the end of a new reed next to it pointing inwards and go on working. The rest of the work will hold it in place and the ends may be cut off close to the work when the weaving is finished.

The teapot stand is finished off with one of the simplest borders of all, that known as three-rod plain border. This border is suitable for small articles such as beverage trays or small serving baskets. To work it, squeeze all the stakes in turn with the round-nosed pliers just where the setting up finished. You will probably find it a help to damp the stakes again at this point as the reed will probably have dried while you were working the sides. Study Fig. 4 (A & B) carefully, while you are working. Bend down stake number 1 behind number 2, number 2 behind number 3, and number 3 behind number 4. Pass number 1 over numbers 2 and 3, in front of 4 and behind 5, coming out in front. Bend number 4 down by the side of number 1 so that they lie side by side and not on top of one another. Repeat this process with numbers 2 and 3. Take number 4 in front of number 7, behind number 8 and out to the front. Bend number 7 down to the right of it, as before. This movement is repeated all round. There should always be three pairs projecting and the fifth reed of this set of six (counting from the right) is always the one which is passed in front of the next upright stake, behind the next and out to the front. The left hand reed of each pair is left projecting outwards. Continue until only one stake is left standing upright. Take the fifth reed of the three pairs in front of the upright stake and thread it under the first reed you

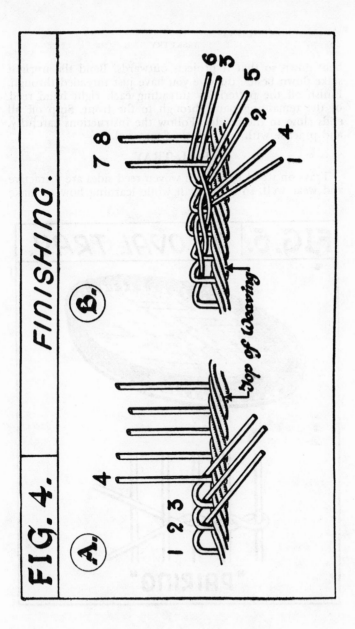

FIG. 4.

FINISHING.

bent down so that it projects outwards. Bend the upright stake down beside the one you have just threaded through. Finish off the pattern by threading each right hand reed of the remaining pairs through to the front. Snip off all ends close to the border. Follow the instructions carefully, and practise with odd pieces of material.

OVAL TRAY

Trays on wood bases with woven reed sides are attractive and wear well, so it is worth while learning how to make

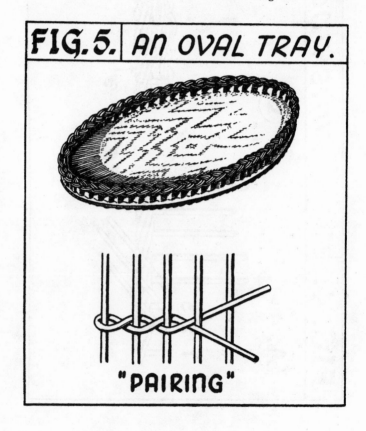

FIG. 5. AN OVAL TRAY.

"PAIRING"

one properly. Round or oval trays are a little easier to work than oblong ones as there are no corners, so we will start with an oval tray measuring say, 16″ x 10″. If you intend to make your own base, cut a paper pattern first, transfer it to the wood by drawing round it with a carpenter's pencil and cut out with a fretsaw or small hacksaw. Sandpaper thoroughly and then drill holes about ½″ apart and ¼″ in from the edge all round. It does not matter whether the number of holes is odd or even.

If the surface of the tray is to be stained or enamelled, do this first and see that it is perfectly dry before the reed sides are added.

Cut the correct number of stakes of No. 2 reed, each about 14″ long, insert in the holes and work a foot border as described for the teapot stand.

The reed used for the weaving in the original was also No. 2 but a narrower could also be used. If finer reed is used, however, you may find it necessary to work an extra row to get the correct depth. This should be about one inch. Pull up the foot border as tightly as possible, then work one row of three-ply coil weave, to make sure that the stakes will remain firmly fixed. The rest of the weaving is done with 'pairing' (see Fig. 5). Squeeze a length of reed to one side of the centre (so that the two sections are uneven and will not both require a new piece of reed at the same time), and slip the loop thus formed over one of the upright stakes. Take the left hand reed over the one on the right and make one stroke behind the next upright stake. Continue in this way all round, always using the left hand reed. Work four complete rows and cut off the end. The tray is now ready for the border, which, in this case, is a simple three stroke braid. If you look carefully at the diagrams, you will see that the braid has two reeds on the outside and three on the inside, all round.

Cut two 3″ lengths of No. 2 reed, and three 8″ lengths. Place one of the short pieces to the right of one of the stakes and bend this stake down over it. Lay one of the 8″ pieces alongside this stake with about 2½″ projecting on the inside, see Fig. 6 (A). Place the second short piece alongside the second stake and bend this down with another 8″

piece by it. Now take the first pair (number 1 stake and
the first spare piece) under the second 3″ piece, over the
second pair and in front of stake number 3, leaving the
ends inside between this stake and the next, see Fig. 6 (B).
Bend number 3 down over the two stakes and lay the third
8″ piece next to it. Take the left hand pair of stakes, which
will be number 2, and the second spare stake and pass it
over number 3 and the third spare stake, and in front of
number 4, again leaving the two ends inside. Bend down
number 4 and then bend down the left hand pair on the
inside beside it, so that the three reeds lie side by side with
number 4 reed on the left of the group, see Fig. 6 (C).
Take the left hand outside pair and pass it over the outside group of three and in front of number 5 and the inside
left pair. You will now have two groups of three on the
outside. Take the two right hand reeds of the left hand
group, pass them over the right hand group of three and
behind the next upright, leaving the left hand reed projecting on the outside. Bend over the upright and continue
in this way all round the tray until the last stake and the
last pair of reeds have been bent down. Remove the first
short piece and in its place put the left hand front pair.
Remove the second spare piece and put the next pair in its
place. You will now have a row of single projecting reeds
on the outside, and on the inside there will be three pairs
pointing to the right and three single reeds pointing to the
left. The single reeds should be shaved to a point and
threaded into place alongside the pairs, and then the right
hand reed of each pair can be threaded into their places
alongside these. All the ends may now be clipped off close
to the border.

OBLONG TRAY (WITH HANDLES)

Cut out the plywood base to the size and shape required
and drill holes all round. Notice that the short sides should
have an uneven number of holes so that there will be one in
the exact centre. Be careful not to put a hole in the corners,
as a better result is obtained if there is a hole on each side
of each corner. Cut enough 14″ stakes from No. 2 reed, to

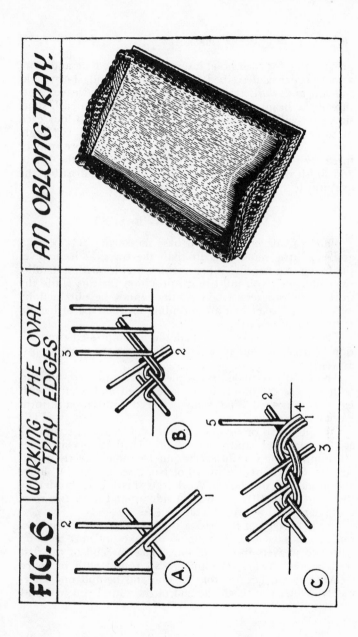

FIG. 6.

WORKING THE OVAL TRAY EDGES

AN OBLONG TRAY.

provide one for each hole, insert them in the base and work a foot border as described for the teapot stand. Turn right side up and work two rows of three-ply coil weave. Now thread the beads on to the seven centre reeds on each short side. You will need two beads about 1" high and four each of three smaller sizes, the smallest being about ½" high. Put the largest in the middle. Now work two more rows of three-ply coil weave, pressing it well down over the beads, and finish off with a two-rod three stroke braid as for the oval tray.

HANDLED OBLONG BASKET

This is made on a wooden base measuring 2½" x 5½" and is a little more difficult than the trays, as it involves the fixing of a handle. When making articles with a handle, remember that you must make provision for this while the work is in progress. Good results cannot be obtained by making the basket first and deciding on the type of handle to be used, afterwards.

The original basket was made on a compressed composition board base, but plywood will answer the purpose just as well.

The handle is made from a piece of No. 10 reed, finished with a piece of coloured enamelled reed and wound with flat wrapping reed. The enamelled reed is also used to form a decorative stripe.

Cut the board or plywood to the required size, round off each corner and sandpaper smooth. Drill twenty-six holes all round, being careful not to put any holes exactly in the corners. Cut twenty-six pieces of No. 2 reed, each 14" long, and insert in the holes. Work the small base border as shown in Fig 2 (B). Turn right side up and work two rows of three-ply coil weave. Cut off the ends.

The main part of the basket is worked in over-and-under, but as you have an even number of stakes, it must be done with two weavers instead of one. Place the end of the first reed between two stakes and go all round with ordinary weaving stitch, i.e., in front of one and behind one alternately. When you reach the end of the round you will find

FIG. 7. OBLONG BASKET.

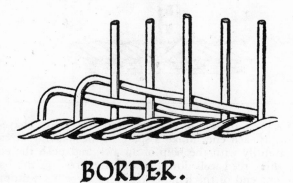

BORDER.

that you will have to go behind two stakes next to one another, so drop this reed and start another one. Continue working with the alternate reeds until you have worked six complete rows. Cut off the last but one reed and, instead, use a piece of flat enamelled reed to work one round. Cut this off and continue working as before for four more rounds. Add a third reed and work one row of three-ply coil weave to make the top firm.

Squeeze the first stake about ½″ above this row and bend over, going behind one, in front of one, behind one and in front of one, leaving the end inside behind the next stake (Fig. 7). Continue in this way all round, working as usual from left to right. When you reach the end, thread the remaining stakes through the first ones bent down, to complete the pattern (Fig. 7). This is a simpler border than that used for the teapot stands or trays, but it gives a lighter appearance and is quite suitable for small baskets

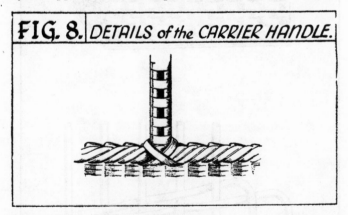

FIG. 8. DETAILS of the CARRIER HANDLE.

Cut a piece of No. 10 15″ long and 'slype,' i.e., shave to a point, at each end. Make a space in the weaving at each side, carefully with the help of an awl, and push the ends of the thick reed well down, so that they rest on the base. Secure one end of the handle with a piece of flat wrapping reed as shown in Fig. 8 but do not cut the end. Lay a piece of the coloured reed along the top of the handle and wind the flat wrapping reed over it, taking one turn under and one turn over the enamelled piece alternately. When you reach the other side of the handle, cut off the coloured reed, and secure the end of the wrapping reed to match the first side.

ARTICLES MADE ON A REED BASE

We come now to a branch of basketry which, while a little more difficult to work, widens our scope enormously. Baskets made on a reed base are, of course, much more practical than those made on a wooden one. It is impossible here to describe every type of basket which can be made, but I shall endeavour to lay down the general principles to be followed, since the method is the same in every case, whatever the shape of the basket and purpose for which it is intended. As a general rule, the stakes used in these baskets are of thicker reed than that used for the weaving. This not only makes for a better appearance but assists the worker in keeping the basket a good shape. Always make up your mind what shape you want your basket to be before you start it. Decide, too, on just what type of handle you require, and remember to make provision for it, while you are working the sides.

SET OF TABLE MATS IN REED

A set of round mats in three sizes, measuring respectively 7″, 9″ and 12″, can be made quite quickly and will wear well. The size can, of course, be adjusted quite easily by working more or fewer rounds of weaving. For the small mat you will need ten pieces of reed (No. 2) each 10″ long for the stakes, and several lengths of finer reed, for the weaving. Start by slitting five of the stakes for about 1″, in the centre of each. This is quite easy if a small sharp pen-knife is used and if you go slowly. Thread these five reeds on to the centre of the sixth, then thread the other four reeds through the slits so that the stakes form a cross as shown in Fig 9.

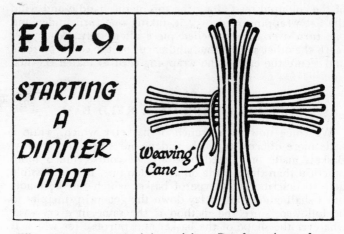

FIG. 9.

STARTING A DINNER MAT

Weaving Cane

The mats are worked in pairing. Bend a piece of very fine reed in half and slip over one of the arms of the cross. Be careful to keep the arms at right angles while working the first few rounds, as a mistake made now will be difficult to rectify later on. Work two rounds of pairing, treating each group of five stakes as one. Now divide each group into three, putting a single reed in the centre, with a group of two on each side. As you work pull the stakes apart, so that they are as nearly equidistant as possible, treating each group of two as a single stake. Work three rows of pairing on these stakes, then divide the pairs again into single stakes. Continue in pairing, keeping the stakes as evenly divided as possible, until the mat measures just over five inches across. Keep the pairing reeds unequal in length so that you will not need to join a new one to each piece at the same time.

The mats are finished off with a simple scalloped border. This is worked as shown in Fig. 10 (A). Bend one stake over to the right, taking it in front of one stake and tucking it down alongside the left hand side of the next. In order to get the scallops even, pull this stake out and measure it, then cut all the other stakes to the same length. Shave each one to a point and work the border.

A slightly more elaborate border can be worked as shown in Fig. 10 (B). These two borders are suitable for mats and small baskets, but should not be used on larger articles as they are inclined to spring out.

The larger mats are made in exactly the same way as the smaller one, but the stakes are cut 12″ and 16″ in length respectively. Should the mats appear slightly frayed when they are finished, the thin fibres may be removed by being passed through a low flame.

ROUND WORK BASKET

The base of this basket is made in exactly the same way as the flat round mats. Cut ten pieces of medium reed, each piece 7″ long, and arrange them in the form of a cross exactly as you did for the mats. Take a length of fine reed, bend into a loop and slip it over one arm of the cross. Work in pairing, dividing the stakes into 'twos and ones' after the second round, and into single stakes after the fifth round. Continue working until the work is about 5″ across. Bend the stakes away from you as you work, so that the bottom of the basket is slightly curved.

Cut off all the stakes close to the weaving. There is no need to cut off the weaving stakes now. Cut forty 16″ lengths of the medium width, and sharpen one end of each to a point about ¾″ long. Push one stake into the base on each side of each stake as far as it will go. Make the space required with the aid of your awl. You will probably find that pushing the stakes into place has also pushed down the weaving a little so that the stakes in the base are showing, so work another row of pairing all round over all the stakes, treating each group of three as one stake.

Now squeeze each stake with the round-nosed pliers close to the edge of the weaving and bend it up. Bend a length of fine reed in half, and slip it over one of the upright stakes next to the two pairing reeds. You will now have four lengths projecting from four adjacent spaces, ready to begin the first row of four-ply coil weave. This is worked in exactly the same way as the three-ply coil weave, except that each reed goes in front of three stakes instead of in

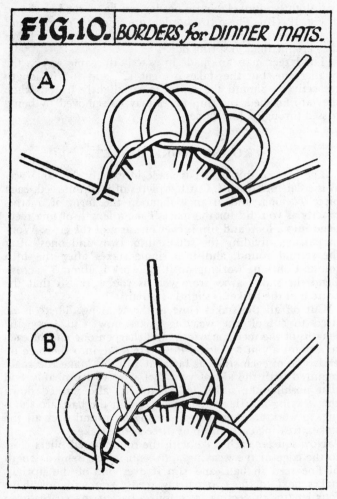

FIG. 10. BORDERS for DINNER MATS.

A

B

front of two. The rest of the stroke, i.e., behind one and out to the front again, is continued all round until you reach the beginning of the row— when the last used reed comes out in the same place as the first. Take this reed in front of three stakes, behind one and out to the front and cut it off. Do the same with the next three, starting from the right hand side, but do not cut these off. You are now ready to work three rows of three-ply coil weave. So far, you will have been working with the basket resting on your knee or on the table, but once the stakes are set, it is easier and quicker to work on a board, so that both hands are free to manipulate the weaving. Gently prise apart the stakes in the base, and peg the basket to the work board in such a way that it will revolve easily.

Keep the stakes at equal distances apart, and work six rows of pairing, pressing each row well down as you go along. The original basket had sides which curved out a little at the base and then went up straight, but if you wish your basket to have sloping sides, you must shape them as you work. After the six rows of pairing come two rows of three-ply coil. When these two rows are done, cut the ends and work one row of over-and-under using flat wrapping reed or enamelled reed in a contrasting colour. Work one row of pairing with the fine reed, then another row of over-and-under with the coloured reed, going in front of and behind the same stakes as in the previous over-and-under. Work two more rows of three-ply coil, four of pairing and two more of three-ply coil. Damp the stakes and work one of the borders already described. In the original, this was a three-rod plain border, but a braided border would look just as well, particularly if you intend to give the basket a top of gathered material. Cut off all the ends of reed close to the work.

LINING THE BASKET

The original basket was lined with silk to match the coloured reed. Cut a ring of cardboard to fit the base and cut a large hole in it, so that it will lie flat. Cover with padding and a circle of silk cut to fit. Cut a piece of material long enough to go all round the inside of the basket, allowing one inch or so for turnings, and as deep as the basket plus 12″ for turnings and the gathered top. Seam the sides and make a two-inch hem along one side; with two rows of stitching, leaving a slot each side to take the drawstring. Gather along the raw edge, place lining in basket with the padded circle over the raw edge and stitch all round the base, taking the stitches through to the outside and round the stakes. Be careful to stitch both lining and pad at the same time. Put a row of stitching all round, just under the border, to keep the lining in place, again being careful to go round the reed stakes and not through them.

Thread two pieces of matching cord through the hem at the top, and tie on opposite sides. If pockets are required in the basket, they must, of course, be stitched to the lining before this is put into the basket. If desired, the sides of the basket may be lightly padded.

LIDDED BASKET

The basket part is made in exactly the same way as for the one without a lid but the lining, of course, is turned in and stitched just under the border. Start making the lid just as you did the base of the basket, but when the base measures about four inches across, add one bi-stake to the side of each stake already there. These bi-stakes should be about 5″ long. Continue with the pairing, separating out and using the stakes singly, so that you have forty instead of the original twenty. Curve the stakes a little as you work, as a slightly domed lid fits better than a perfectly flat one. When the lid measures one inch less than the top of the basket, work two rows of three-ply coil to give extra strength. Cut off all stakes close to the last row of weaving. Cut forty pieces of the fine width, each 10″ long. Push one piece in beside each stake. Use these to work a three-rod plain border. Pad and line the lid to match the lining of the basket.

The directions given here for making the basket can, of course, be varied at the desire of the workers. Endless variations in the arrangement of the various types of weaving and the shape and size of the basket are possible. It is probably true to say that no two baskets need ever be exactly alike.

All round baskets on a reed base are made as I have just described. In the next chapter, I shall deal with the question of handles, the addition of which will turn our work baskets into shopping baskets.

CHAPTER III

Handles: Importance — types — methods — wrapped handles — alternatives — cores. **More Weaving Patterns:** Chain pairing — arrow weaves — fitching — double stake borders — variation — four-rod plain border — wrapped borders. **Final Hints:** Correct size reed — general rule — simplicity of design — alternative materials — regularity — — practise.

HANDLES

ONE of the most important features of a basket, whether it is made from reed, willow or rush, is the handle. A handle must be strong enough to take the weight of whatever is carried in the basket and it should be in keeping with the general design of the article of which it forms part. A handle can also be decorative, although it must be suitable too.

There are many types of handles and many different ways of decorating them, although the majority are fixed to the basket in very much the same way. The reed used for handles is generally No. 7 or No. 10 according to the size of the basket, and the piece used is known as the bow. Cut the reed to the length required—do not forget to allow for the ends which will be pushed into the sides of the basket—and bend it to the shape of a bow, tying the ends with a piece of string to keep them in place. Soak it, so that it is pliable. Point each end for about two inches, or longer, if the basket is wide and deep, and push one end very firmly into each side of the basket as far as it will go, making a space for it by cutting with an awl. In making large baskets, it is a good idea to push a piece of reed of the same size into place when you are working the sides. This can be removed when the basket is finished, and the handle reed pushed in its place. Handles should never be put in before the weaving is worked, as it is very difficult to work the weaving if this is done and, when the border is reached, extra reeds have to be inserted to take the place of those used for the handle.

On large baskets, the reed should be pegged in place. There are two ways of doing this. The first is to make a hole in the side of the handle reed just under the top weaving. A pointed peg of thinner reed is thrust through the hole and acts as a peg, the ends being hidden by the border.

The second method is to make a hole in the reed going from front to back, again, just under the top. Point a piece of wrapping reed and push the end through the hole. The short end is then tucked into the weaving and the other end brought to the front under the top weaving, at the left, crossed over to the right, taken down and up through the weave from the back, over and down on the left of the handle, to form a cross (see Fig. 11).

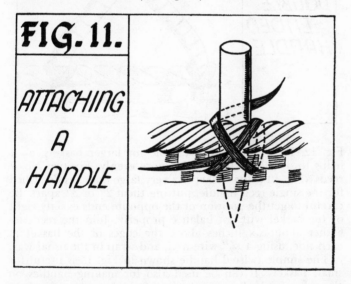

FIG. 11.

ATTACHING A HANDLE

If the handle is to be a wrapped one, the wrapping reed is not cut off but used to cover the bow by winding it closely and firmly round until the other side is reached. Here the end is pointed and threaded through the basket to form a cross and match the first side. Use a long piece of wrapping reed, so that there will be no need to join it on the handle.

A decorative effect can be obtained by laying a piece of flat reed in a contrasting colour, over the bow. When wrapping the handle, take alternate rows under and over this piece. Various patterns can be worked out, according to the number of turns taken over the contrasting piece.

An attractive method of making handles is shown in

FIG. 12.

A DOUBLE ~ENDED HANDLE.

Fig. 12. It is particularly suitable for larger baskets, as it helps to distribute the weight more evenly. Fix two No. 7 reeds (No. 10 if the basket is a very large one), as described for the single reed handle, putting them 2″ or 3″ apart. Be careful to get the position of the opposite ends exactly right or the basket will not balance properly. Join the reeds together about six inches above the edges of the basket at each side, using a ½″ wire nail, and wrap in the usual way.

The simple twisted handle shown in Fig. 13 is useful for small baskets. It can be used also for making handles on the side of a basket (e.g., a clothes basket), or to make a looped fastening for the lid of a workbasket. In the latter case, of course, the ends would be much nearer together. Insert a length of reed (medium size), just under the border. Twist the ends together evenly and firmly, until the handle is the correct length. Thread the ends through under

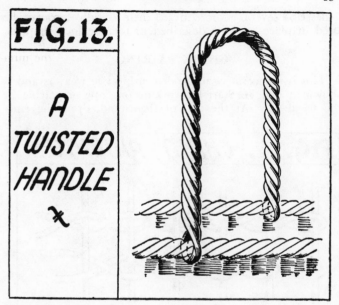

FIG.13.

A TWISTED HANDLE

x

the border at the other side of the basket going in opposite directions. Finish off one end by taking it into the weaving for a few strokes, and twist the other round the handle again, so that all three reeds are twisted evenly. Finish off by taking a few strokes into the weaving, and cutting off the end.

This method is only suitable for small baskets, but can be used for larger ones if a 'core' of No. 7 or No. 10 reed is put into the basket first. The three thinner reeds are then wound over this. This method is one which is often used for the handles of baskets woven from willow rods.

MORE WEAVING PATTERNS

The weaving strokes or patterns, and the methods of working borders already described, should be sufficient to enable the beginner to work many kinds of baskets and other articles. It may, however, be of help and interest if

I describe several more. Any of these could, of course, be used in place of those described in the previous chapters.

CHAIN PAIRING

This is a decorative method of using two weavers and is shown in Fig. 14. Start by working one row of pairing in the usual way At the end of the round, draw the ends

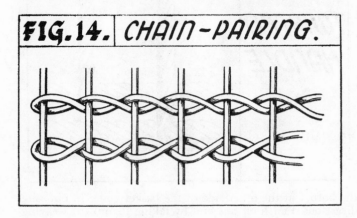

FIG. 14. CHAIN-PAIRING.

through to the front and cut them off. Bend a length of reed in half and slip over one of the stakes, preferably a little farther on, so that you do not have too many ends in the same place. Let the ends come out at the front in two adjacent spaces. Take the left hand reed in front of one stake and under the right hand reed and behind the next stake to the front again. Continue in this way, always using the left hand reed until the end of the row is reached. Draw the ends through and cut them off. When a band of chain pairing is required, the two methods are used alternately.

ARROW WEAVES

An interesting arrow effect in weaving can be achieved by doing a row of regular pairing (using weavers in two colour if you like) and then weaving a reverse row above

it with the pattern going in the opposite direction. For the
first row, bring the left weaver out from under the other
weaver and cross it over the second one before passing it
behind the next stake. For the reverse pairing, bring the
weaver out from above the other weaver and cross it *under*
the second before passing it behind the next stake. Follow
this procedure exactly, as any deviation or irregularity will
be evident in the arrow pattern.

A double two-tone pairing arrow may be made in the
same way, except that you hold two weavers of each colour
parallel and use them as one to weave the alternate rounds
of regular and reverse pairing. A three-ply rod or Indian
arrow pattern is done by placing a reverse triple twist or
three-ply coil above a regular three-ply coil.

FITCHING OR FETCHING

This is a method of working an open border or stripe.
The simplest method is to leave a space of say an inch of
stakes uncovered between two rows of pairing. Bi-stakes—

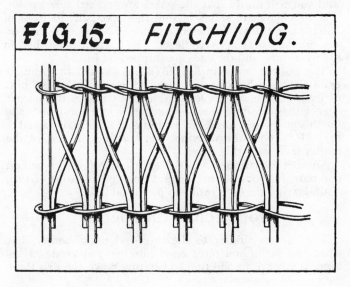

one on each side of each of the original stakes—may be added to give additional strength. A pretty openwork effect, such as that shown in Fig. 15, is obtained by placing a bi-stake on each side of those in the basket. Each bi-stake is then crossed over the one nearest to it and held in place by a row of twisted pairing. This is worked with two reeds in the usual way, but an additional twist is made between each stroke, in order to hold the bi-stakes close together.

DOUBLE STAKE BORDERS

In these borders, strokes are each made with two stakes instead of one. The additional stakes, which must be of the same thickness as the main stakes in the basket, are pushed into the weaving by the side of the original ones. All the stakes should be about 4″ above the three-ply coil weaving, or a little longer if a thick reed is used. In starting a row for such a border, you must bend the first stake down about 5/8″ above the weaving, to allow for the threading in of the final stakes. Fig. 16 (A) shows a simple double stake border and you will notice that the stakes are worked side by side. Take each pair of stakes behind the next pair, in front of the next two, leaving the ends inside. The edge of the border must be kept perfectly level. The pattern is finished in the usual way, and the ends are snipped off inside.

The border shown in Fig. 16 (B), is worked in a similar manner but each pair goes in front of one pair, behind one, in front of one, and is left inside. This makes the border deeper than the previous one and allowance must be made for this at the beginning, by bending the first pair of stakes over 1⅛″ above the weaving, and keeping the rest of the border level with this.

Another variation is to take each pair of stakes behind one pair, in front of two, behind one and in front of two, again leaving the ends inside to be cut off later.

FOUR-ROD PLAIN BORDER

This is very similar to the three-rod plain border, but when you begin you must bend number 4 stake down behind number 5, in addition to bending down the first three

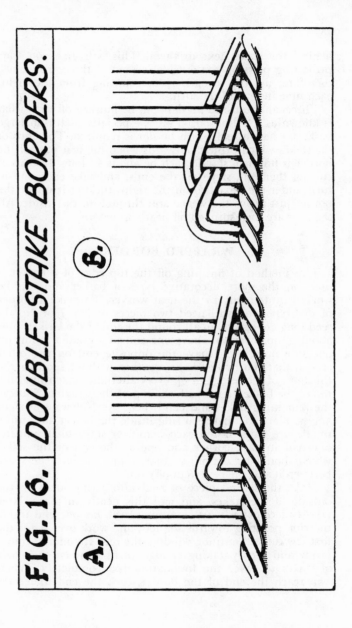

FIG. 16. DOUBLE-STAKE BORDERS.

A.

B.

behind the stake next to them. This will give you four projecting pairs on the outside instead of three. You must, therefore, use the seventh reed, counting from the right, each time instead of the fifth.

Three- and four-rod borders can be finished off with what is known as a 'follow-on.' This is especially useful on large baskets, where a really firm border is required. The ends of the stakes which project outwards when the first part of the border is finished, should each be about 4″ long. Instead of cutting them off, slype all the ends, and take each one in turn under the next two on the right, tucking it under the border just above the weave and through to the inside. All the ends are then snipped off neatly as before.

WRAPPED BORDERS

This method of finishing off the top edge of a basket is used on the more decorative type of basket and can be worked quite easily by the neat worker. To make a border of this type, you will need two pieces of No. 7 or No. 10 reed long enough to go all round the top of the basket, plus about 3″ for overlap. Shave one end to a gradual point on one side only, then shave the opposite end on the other end so that the two ends fit together without spoiling the thickness of the reed. Cut off every alternate stake round the top of the basket, level with the top of the weaving. Squeeze the remaining stakes and bend them over sideways at right angles. Place the first reed ring inside the basket and, using small wire nails, fasten each bent-over stake to it, putting one nail in each corner and one at the end of the stake, which should be cut off, so that it just fits into the space between it and the next (cut-off) one.

Make the second piece of reed into a ring to fit on the outside of the stakes, and nail this neatly in place. Now take a piece of ordinary wrapping reed, lay one end inside the rim, pointing towards the left, and work over it for the first few turns. Continue winding the reed round and round firmly and evenly, taking enough turns between each pair of stakes to cover the foundation rod completely. When you reach the end of the border, tuck the end under the last turn, pull tight, and cut off. A nail on the inside will make it quite secure.

FINAL HINTS

Before I leave the subject of reed basketry, here are a few hints which will help you to get the best results from your work.

First, there is the question of the correct size of reed to use for a particular purpose. As a general rule, the larger the basket you propose to make, the thicker the reed you use should be.

Avoid the use of the same size reed for both stakes and weaving, as this makes it difficult to keep the stakes a good shape.

Always press one row of weaving as close to the one beneath as possible, as this makes the work both look and wear better.

Avoid the use of too many types of weaving in any one article. Simplicity of design and evenness of working will produce the best results. Simple pairing or over-and-under broken only by a row of three-ply coil weave, or a stripe in a contrasting colour, looks better than several patterns in the same basket, however much such a basket may show off your skill and versatility.

Braided rush or raffia or Hong Kong grass can add interest to your work, but when you do include such materials, keep the actual weaving very simple. Over-and-under is the best stroke to use, providing you are careful to see that your upright stakes are really strong ones, capable of resisting the pull of the thicker weavers.

Aim always at regularity in your work. This will come only with repeated practise, so do not be discouraged if your first efforts are not as even as you would like. Familiarity will bring ease in the handling of your material.

Finally, do not attempt too much all at once. Reed is not a particularly easy material to handle, and too much work at once can be extremely tiring. Start with the thinnest reeds and work up gradually to the thicker and more difficult ones.

A SELECTION OF BASKETS, OLD AND NEW

1, 2, 3. Baskets made by the Mission Indians of California.

4. Coiled beaded basket from the Pomo tribe of California.

5. Storage basket with intricate spiral pattern made by the Pomo Indians of California.

6. Deep storage basket made by the Haida tribe.

7. Long coiled basket from the Narragansett Indians of Rhode Island.

8. Basket, 12⅛ inches high, made by the Seri Indians of Mexico.

9. Diegueno Indian basket made at Manzanita, California.

10. Basket made by Diegueno Indians at San Diego, California.

11. Basket with a coiled snake pattern made by Diegueno Indians.

12, 13. Basketry weaves used by the Esmeraldos Indians of Ecuador.

14, 15, 16. Weaves reproduced from prehistoric woven articles found by American archaeologists in the caves of Kentucky, believed to have been made from such materials as cattail fibres, tree barks, corn husks and grasses.

17, 18. Baskets woven of grass for holding toilet articles, made in Thebes about 2,000 B.C.

19, 20. Useful and decorative baskets made by modern American craftsmen.

21. Baskets by contemporary New England craftsmen, made of (l. to r.) pine roots, brown ash, palm leaves and birch bark.

1

2

3

4

5

6

7

8

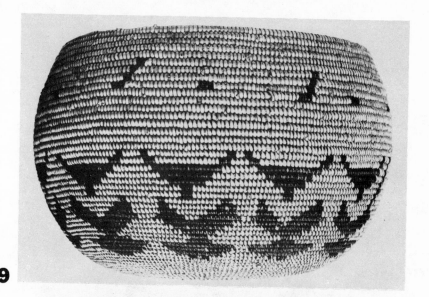

9

10

11

12

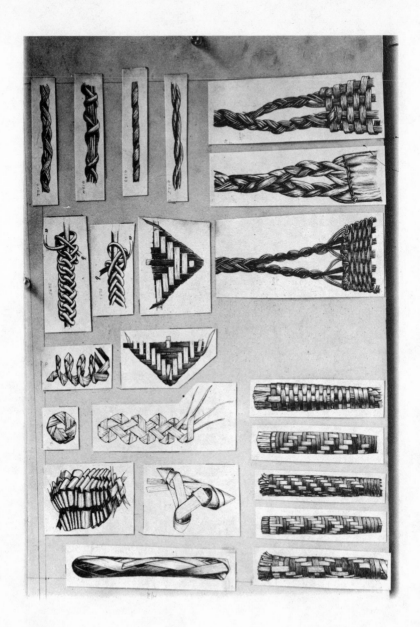

13

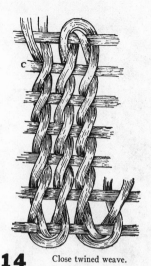

14 Close twined weave.

15 Twined weave showing chevron pattern.

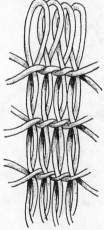

-Open twined weave.

16

17

18

20

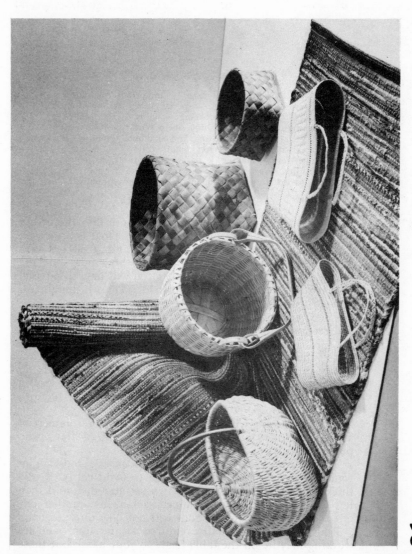

Willow Basketry: Utility class — important differences — preparation — wetting — special tools. **Willow Bicycle Basket:** Oval base — working — joins — side stakes — working the sides — finishing. **Skein Work:** Easier handling — special tools — splitting and shaving — joining. **Basketry with Plastic Wire:** Small trays and baskets — properties — making a basket — working sequence — finishing. **Waste Basket:** Lucite base. **A Napkin Ring:** Useful article — commencing — working — practise.

WILLOW BASKETRY

WILLOW baskets may be said to come more into the utility class than those made from reed, although that is no reason why they should not be both well-made and attractive. Willow basketry is not particularly easy on the hands, since the rods are strong and springy, so that you will be well advised to leave it alone until you have had a certain amount of practise with the more pliable reed.

There are several important differences between willow and reed and these, naturally, affect the way in which they are used. In the first place, willow is very much shorter and stiffer and, therefore, as I have already pointed out, not nearly so easy to work with. Then, too, the rods vary in size owing to the fact that they are used more or less in their natural state in which, of course, they taper off to a point at the top.

In this country willow is used primarily for commercial articles, such as clothes hampers, rather than by those who pursue basketry as a home craft.

To prepare willows for working, soak the rods under water until they are pliable enough to bend easily. Really thick rods should be soaked for two or three days and then left under a piece of well-damped sacking for another day or so. Smaller and thinner rods will not take quite so long.

Rods which are actually required at the time you are working may lie on the table ready to your hand, but those not wanted immediately should be left under the damp cloth until you need them. You will find that willows dry very quickly when they are exposed to the air, particularly if you are working in a warm room. If the rods with which you are working or those already in the basket become dry, dip them in water and leave them to drain. Any unfinished work may be left under the damp cloth until you are ready to go on with it.

Willow is much tougher on the hands and much harder to cut than reed so you will need a pair of special shears, and also a knife with a broad blade, sharpened only along one end. It is used for cutting off the ends of the rods when the weaving is finished. Because of the manual strength needed, more men than women go in for willow basketry.

Willow-work is 'messier' than ordinary reed work, and it is difficult to do it in an ordinary room where there are other people, as it requires a lot of space. A work board such as that recommended for reed work, should be used.

The actual methods of weaving, setting and bordering, adding stakes, and so on, are exactly the same as those used for reed basketry. Many willow baskets contain both brown and white rods and the contrast between the two gives a very decorative effect. Handles are fixed to willow baskets in the manner described in the chapter on this part of the work, although the twisted type of handle is more generally used than the more decorative wrapped type.

WILLOW BICYCLE BASKET

This basket is made on an oval base and is fastened to the handle bars of the bicycle by means of two small straps inserted under the weaving and border. The oval base is one we have not attempted as yet, but it is made on the same principle as the circular base used for the table mats, and is quite simple to do if care is taken. Incidentally, if you want to make a set of oval dinner mats, you would start them in just the same way as you start the bicycle basket.

To make the oval base, you will need nine sticks cut from the thicker or 'butt' end of the rods. These sticks should be, as nearly as possible, the same thickness as one

FIG. 17. | A WILLOW BICYCLE BASKET

Bicycle Basket

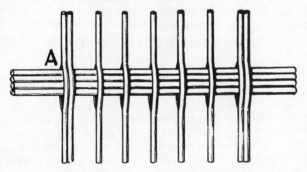

A

Starting the Base

another. Slit each rod in the middle with a sharp penknife for about ¼″. Be careful not to let this slit extend too far, or the other sticks will not be held firmly. Cut four pieces each 14″ long, and slide these through the smaller pieces as shown in Fig. 17. Take two lengths of willow of approximately the same thickness and push the top ends—these are, of course, where the rod is thinnest—into the slit rod at the point marked 'A' in Fig. 17. If the ends are thin and ragged, cut off a few inches. Work one row of pairing all round, keeping the stakes quite straight and twisting the weavers as tightly as possible. Press each stroke close to the foundation stakes.

On the next round separate the four end stakes into two groups of two, and work one more round. Now work two more rounds, separating all the pairs into single stakes (including the short stakes at each end). Work three more rounds on the single stakes, then shave the ends of the pairing stakes and tuck them under the previous row of pairing.

As the willow rods are comparatively short, you will be obliged to have rather more joins than you have in reed-work. To join on a new rod, simply let the end of the old rod project outwards, leaving it to be cut off later, and lay the new one alongside it with the end pointing inwards, and away from you. When the old end is the top of the rod lay the top of the next rod against it. When you reach the end of this rod, of course, you will find that it is the butt end, so lay the butt end of the new rod against it, and go on working. This method of joining evens up the weaving and prevents a sudden change from thin to thick rods.

The base of the basket should now measure about 11″ x 4″ and is ready for staking-up. This is the process by which the stakes you are going to use as a foundation for the sides, are inserted. Cut off all the bottom stakes with your shears or a very sharp knife, just close enough to the weaving to allow the outer rods of the pairing to rest on them. When the stakes are cut they must be 'picked,' i.e., cut off at an angle of about 45 degrees. Note that your shears and knife must be really sharp as the willow is tough and apt to splinter.

When making larger oval baskets in this way, it is usual
to work several rows in ordinary pairing, and the rest in
reversed pairing, in order to counteract a tendency to twist.
A twisted base can never be pulled straight after it is
worked. Reverse pairing is worked in the same way as ordinary pairing, but is done from front to back instead of
from back to front. Each rod is kept at the back of the
work and is brought forward in turn, passing in front of
the next stake, over the right hand weaving rod and through
to the back again.

Cut twenty-six rods from the butt ends, each 18″ long,
slype the ends and insert one stake at the right hand side
of each bottom stake, pushing each one well down into the
weaving. The stakes must now be bent upwards to form the
sides of the basket. Hold each stake in turn in the left
hand, and put the point of a sharp penknife into the rod
just beyond the edge of the base. As the left hand bends the
stake up, give the knife a sharp half-turn, so that the stake
will kink but not crack. The stakes will fall down again as
soon as you loose them, but this will not matter. The technical name for this process is 'pricking-up.' Gather up the
stakes into a hoop made from a spare rod twisted into an
oval, then tap each bend gently with a chisel or iron rod,
to make sure that the stake is firmly fixed in the base. If
necessary, work an extra row of pairing all round, so that
the ends of the bottom stakes are completely covered.

Take three thin rods and insert them between the up-
rights in three adjacent spaces, ready to begin the base
border. Work three rows of three-ply coil weave, joining
tops to tops and butts to butts, as before. Change to over-
and-under, using a fresh rod for each round as you have
an even number of stakes. Start the first row with a butt
and the next with a top and so on. As you work, let the
stakes slope out a little, but not too much. Be careful to see
that the stakes are not allowed to become corrugated by
the pull of the weaving. You will find that the weavers will
kink as they go round the stakes and this is an advantage,
since it makes the weaving of the finished basket tight and
resilient. Take care, however, to see that the kink comes in
the right place, immediately in front of or behind one of

the upright stakes. Do not work loosely and then try to pull the rods into place, as this naturally causes them to kink in the wrong place.

Work 2½" or 3" of over-and-under—the exact size is difficult to determine owing to variations in the thickness of the rods—work two more rows of three-ply coil weaving, then 2" or 3" of over-and-under. Work two more rows of three-ply coil weave to set the stakes, then work a three-rod plain border. Damp the stakes well first, so that they will be pliable and so easier to work. Cut off all the ends neatly. Make two spaces in the weaving at the back of the basket, and slip two short buckled straps through, so that the basket can be fixed to the handle bars of the bicycle.

SKEIN WORK

Skein work is a branch of willow basketry which makes an appeal to those workers who find ordinary rod work to be too hard on the hands. Skeins are made from either white or buff rods and are really only thin reeds made by splitting the rod. The skeins are started by making slits in the butt end of the rod with a sharp penknife. The end of the cutter is then placed in the slits and the rod is drawn along so that it is divided into strips. The cutter must be guided carefully so that the skeins will all be the same size.

The next process is that of shaving. Start in the centre of the strip and draw the butt end through the shave, then turn the rod round and repeat the process along the top end. The skeins are now ready for use.

The stakes used in the baskets made from skeins are, of course, the usual ones made from the uncut willow rods. The bases of baskets made in this way are usually worked in what is known as flat skein work. In this, skeins are used so that each row lies as flat as possible on the row beneath, so that when the work is finished, only the edges of each skein can be seen. The sides of the basket are worked in what is known as edge-skein work, and for this the skeins are worked edge to edge in the same way as flat wrapping reed. When joining skeins in this type of work, you must proceed a little differently, for, instead of crossing one rod over the other, you must lay the end of the new piece over the end of the old one and use them together for two or three strokes. The ends are afterwards cut off.

Skeins are often used in the same way as flat wrapping reed, for binding the handles used on willow baskets, or for making wrapped borders.

BASKETRY WITH PLASTIC WIRE

Plastic covered wire can be used for weaving small trays or baskets and, if well done in attractive colours, accords well with modern taste and schemes of decoration. It is clean and wears well and is easy to handle. It is an excellent material for children's projects in crafts classes and summer camps.

Plastic wire can be obtained from craft supply stores at very low prices. Colours are usually bright and clear, and the wire is also obtainable in black and white. Some of it is made from rayon or cotton covered with a thin plastic coating and is clean, flexible and easy to handle.

One disadvantage it has in comparison with reed, is that it is much heavier and is, therefore, unsuitable for larger articles such as shopping baskets.

Tray and teapot stand sides can be made from the medium size, but to give the most pleasing results from an artistic point of view, the bases should be of some kind of plastic material such as plexiglas, which will easily resist the normal heat given out by a teapot or similar article.

The small basket shown in Fig. 18 could be used for holding a spray of flowers, either dried everlasting flowers, or artificial ones, made from such things as fir cones, beech nuts, acorns, etc., or from self hardening clay. The addition of a small round tin enamelled to match the plastic wire will turn it into a useful ashtray, with enough weight in it to prevent its being overturned. If the basket is required for an ashtray, it could be made a little smaller, by not working so many rows of weaving in the sides.

The original basket was made on a woven base, but would look just as well with a base made from plexiglas.

FIG. 18.

THINGS to MAKE with PLASTIC WIRE

Small Basket.

Napkin Ring.

Starting the ring.

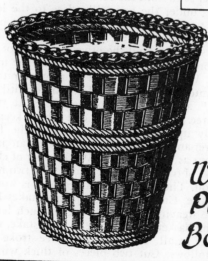

Waste Paper Basket.

In this case you would, of course, drill holes all round to take the wire stakes, and work a foot border in the ordinary way.

To make the basket you will need about four yards of thick or medium wire for the stakes, and about 22 yards of thin wire for the weaving. You may like to use contrasting colours for the basket, although personally, I prefer one colour for this type of thing. Plastic wire can be cut quite easily with scissors, although you will find a pair of wire cutting pliers an advantage, when you come to snipping off the ends, as they will enable you to get closer to the weaving.

Owing to the fact that plastic wire cannot be split in the same way as reed, the method used for making the base is a little different.

Cut eight pieces of the thicker wire, each 10" long. Lay four of the pieces side by side with the ends even and loop a piece of thin wire of a convenient length round them, ready to begin the pairing. This loop should be about one inch to the left of the centre of the wires, and it must be twisted very firmly so as to hold the four wires in place. Lay the other four wires under the first four, close to the loop and at right angles to the other wires. Work the next pairing stroke very firmly round these four, then make two more pairing strokes going round the other two arms of the cross. Work one more two of pairing, then divide the fours into groups of two. Work three rows of pairing over these pairs, then divide into single stakes and continue until the base measures 2½" across. Bend up the stakes at right angles and work three rows of three-ply coil weave, keeping the work absolutely upright, in order to make the foot. Now change to over-and-under and work about an inch, sloping the stakes out as you go round. Work a row of chain pairing, several rows of over-and-under and finally two more rows of three-ply coil. The border, a braided one, is worked with the thinner wire. Cut off all the upright stakes level with the top of the weaving, and push one ten-inch length of thin wire into the basket on each side of each stake, making thirty-two stakes in all. The three-rod three-stroke border is worked as follows: Cut two pieces of thick wire 3" long and six extra pieces of thin wire 10" long. It is a great help if the smaller pieces are a different colour from the weaving stakes, as they can be seen more easily when you come to the end of the braid. Place one small piece between two of the stakes and bend the first stake, which is on the left of it, over. Place two of the spare wires by the side of this bent-over stake, so that about 2½" projects on the inside of the basket. Put the second short piece in the space between the bent-over stake and the next—it is a help if this short piece is allowed to rest on the three wires on its left—and bend over the second stake. Lay two more 10" wires by the side of this stake. Now take the left hand group of three and pass it over the right hand group and in front of the third upright stake, leaving the ends inside. Bend the third stake down, and place the last two spare wires by the side of it, as before. Again take the left hand group, pass it over the next and behind the fourth stake, leaving the ends inside. (You will now have two groups of three inside.) Bend down the fourth stake over the right hand group, then take the left hand inside group and bend it down by the side of the stake. Take the left hand outside group, pass it over the last four bent down, and behind the next upright stake. You will now have two groups of four wires at the front. From now on, only three of these wires are required for each stroke, so always leave the left hand wire of each group on the outside, and take the three right hand ones over the four wires on its left and behind the next upright stake. The extra wire is cut off, when the border is complete.

Continue working all round—three wires over four, bend stake down and bring the three inside wires beside it, each time—and when the beginning is reached, remove the short pieces and thread the last wires under the stakes in their places, to complete the pattern. You will notice that the extra 10" stakes are threaded in pairs from right to left, while the last stakes from the border go from left to right. When the braid is completed, cut off all the ends and press the braid well down, so that it rests on the weaving at an angle of about 45 degrees.

When making say, a large shallow basket to be used for

fruit or cakes, it is advisable to work in the same way as
described for making the lid of the reed workbasket, adding
bi-stakes when the base measures about 4″ or 5″ across.
Always use the thickest wire for anything with a base larger
than 6″.

WASTE PAPER BASKET

A really solid scrap basket, which will not be easily upset,
can be made as shown in Fig. 18. A piece of lucite measuring 8″ in diameter was used in the original, and the stakes
were made 23″ long. Work an ordinary foot border to
secure the stakes. The base could, of course, be made in the
same way as an ordinary reed base. Use thin wire for the
weaving and medium wire for the base. When the base
measures about 8″ across, cut off the stakes and insert
thicker wire for the sides. Whichever base you prefer, the
sides are worked in exactly the same way. Work six rows
of three-ply coil weave to make the base perfectly firm. The
next part of the basket is made from ½″ plastic lacing
bought by the yard, and worked in over-and-under. The
best way to do this part of the work is to cut the lacing to
the length required, plus one inch. Join the ends into a
circle, using a small bifurcated rivet and slip over the
stakes, taking it in front of one and behind the next all
round. Note that in this article it is absolutely essential to
have an odd number of stakes. This is easy to arrange if
the basket has a lucite base, but if it has a woven base, an
extra stake must be inserted between two of the others,
when the work is ready for the setting up.

Work two rows of pairing, then another row of lacing
and continue until the basket is about six inches high.
Work three rows of three-ply coil weave, then several more
rows of alternate pairing and lacing. Finish with three more
rows of three-ply and work a flat braid, this time using the
upright stakes in the usual way.

As I mentioned before, shopping baskets are apt to be
too heavy when plastic wire is used for them, but there are
several smaller articles for which this material is very suitable. Table mats, made in exactly the same way as those

described in an earlier chapter for making reed mats, wear well and keep clean. Make them from the thinnest variety of wire and finish with a scalloped border.

NAPKIN RING

This useful little article looks most attractive when made from the thinnest plastic wire, although ordinary reed in about No. 0, or narrow flat wrapping reed can also be used. It is a good way of using up odd lengths of material, as each ring takes only about two yards of wire or reed. Plastic wire keeps clean longer, and is a little easier to handle, but whichever material you use, the method is exactly the same. If reed is used, it must be well damped, as otherwise it may kink and break when the ends are being threaded through.

Start by taking a piece of wire or No. 0 reed about two yards long. Make a loop round the fingers and twist the reed as shown in Fig. 18. The loop should be as large as you want your finished ring to be, i.e., about 2″ in diameter. Notice that the loop of reed going round the larger ring is actually much tighter than appears in the illustration, as it must not be noticed in the finished ring. Now take the left hand piece of reed and pass it over the right hand piece, and through the ring, treating the ring as the third strand in an ordinary braid. Continue in this way all round, until the beginning is reached. Now take each reed alongside one of the original strands, being careful to see that it lies first on the inside and then on the outside of the original strand each time. Work another round so that you have two strands of the braid consisting of three reeds each and one strand consisting of only one reed. Thread the ends in and out, alongside this reed, so that the braid is even, and cut off the ends inside.

You may find that you will need a little practise in getting the ring the right size at first, but this is easily adjusted once you have made the first ring.

A wider ring can, of course, be made by making each strand four or even five wires wide, but remember to allow another ¾ yards, for each extra round.

RUSH WORK

RUSHES are bought by the bolt or bundle and cost about $2 per bundle. They are most attractive in colouring, as they vary from pale green to light brown, and this mixture of shades is most decorative.

Like other materials used in basketry, rushes must be soaked before they are ready for use. You will probably find that the ends of the rushes are too thin and ragged to be of much use, so cut them off. Then place the rushes in a tank or bath with enough water to cover them. Leave for about ten minutes, drain off the water, and cover with a damp cloth for twenty-four hours. When using the rushes for braiding, allow the braid to dry before beginning to sew it together.

There are two ways of using rushes. The first is by braiding them and the second by using them singly for weaving in the ordinary way. The distinctive character of the rushes gives a character of its own to articles made from them.

Rushes, whether single or braided, can be used in conjunction with reed. Medium reed or willow rods work well with rushes, as they supply the rigidity which the latter lack. A woven willow base made in the manner described in an earlier chapter can be made first. Set up the stakes for the sides in the usual way, and then weave in the rushes. Willow rods may be used, if preferred, for the setting up, weaving and border, to give extra strength.

Rush braids can be of any thickness according to the

purpose for which they are required and the braid must be kept as even in thickness as possible. Braids which are intended to be sewn together should be thicker than those used in conjunction with reed or willow.

Raffia or thin twine is used for sewing the braids together. A curved and flattened needle similar to a packing or string needle should be obtained if possible, and it is worth while taking the trouble to obtain one of these, for it makes the sewing of the braids very much easier. Rush needles can be obtained in a variety of sizes according to the thickness of the braid you wish to sew.

For the shopping basket shown in Fig. 19, you will need a fairly thin braid, so start by tying six rushes together at their thick end. Choose the rushes carefully so that they are as nearly equal in size as possible. Fasten the end of the string to a firm surface. You will probably find it easier to work out of doors in a yard or garden, as this gives you more space to move backwards as the braid grows, and so obviates the necessity for frequent re-tying. As each rush is used up, add a fresh one, but try not to get all the joins in the same place. At times you may find it necessary to work with three rushes or only one, in order to keep the braid even. When joining on a new rush, place the new one inside the old one and work together for a few turns. Try to keep all ends on the same side of the braid. Cut them all off when the braid is finished.

The amount of braid varies, of course, according to the size you want your finished article to be. It is, however, quite a simple matter to add more if necessary, simply by looping a piece of string round the braid a little away from the work in progress, and hanging up in a convenient place while you add more rushes.

Bind the beginning of the braid very firmly with raffia and tie the ends securely. Fold the braid about 12″ from the end and, starting from the fold, stitch the two rows tgoether firmly. It is a help to work on a flat surface rather than on your lap as this enables you to keep the work flat. When you reach the beginning of the braid, turn the braid round and sew it to the other side of the first section. Continue coiling the braid round and round to form an oval,

| FIG. 19. | RUSH WORK. |

a
Rush
Shopping
Basket.

Rush
Mat.

a
Rush
Log
Basket.

stitching each row to the previous one. The stitches are all on the inside of the basket. When the oval is about four or five inches wide, take the raffia through to the outside, lay the next part of the braid flat on top of the inside of the base and oversew firmly all round. When you reach the end of the round, turn and go back, taking the second row of stitches over the first, to form crosses. These crosses are decorative as well as useful. Take the needle through to the wrong side again, turn up the last row worked so that it is at right angles to the base and continue working round and round, placing one row vertically on the row beneath. Slope out the sides a little. When the basket is as deep as you want it, undo a little of the braid and remove one or two of the rushes, so that the braid gradually narrows. Take the end of the braid very gradually to the inside of the basket, bind the end and sew very securely to the inside of the last row. Make two handles from slightly thicker braids and bind for about an inch at each end, leaving about 2" of braid below the binding. Unravel the ends and trim to form a short stubby tassel. Sew the handles very firmly to the sides of the bag.

A much thicker braid containing twelve rushes, arranged in groups of three, was used for an attractive door mat. Start the braid with single rushes so that the beginning is narrower than the main part will be, and gradually add more until the braid is at least an inch wide. The mat is sewn with thin twine as this wears better than raffia which is apt to fray after the mat has been walked on regularly for a little while. Bind the end and fold about 12" from the end. Sew the two layers together and when you reach the end of the seam, turn the braid round, away from the beginning row. Sew to the other side of the second row and at the end, turn it away from the sewn part again. Continue going up and down in this 'jumping-jack' fashion until the work is about 16" long. When you reach the end of the last row, turn the braid so that it goes along one long side. Stitch in place and continue round the other three sides. Go round and round in this way until the mat is the required size. Thin off the braid at the end and sew securely under the last row.

When making any kind of mat, it is best to work on a table, as this helps to keep the work flat.

Another method which takes rather more materials, but results in a closer thicker mat, is to sew the braids together, with the braided sides facing one another, and only the extreme edges showing in the finished work. A favourite and most attractive way of finishing such a mat is to make a row of small coils, each measuring say, four inches across. These are sewn together in a row so that they just touch and the rest of the mat is sewn round and round in rows. Avoid making coils of this kind too large, as the spaces left are dangerous if they are too big.

Rush mats look very well in halls or kitchens and they need no lining. Regular brushing will keep them free from dust and an occasional quick wash with warm water will keep them clean and fresh. Do not allow them to become soaked, however, as they will take a long time to dry.

Most attractive rustic looking log baskets can be made from braided rushes and they look well in a room furnished in ranch house style. The amount of braid required depends on the size you want your finished basket to be. The basket should be about 12" to 14" high and about 15" or so in diameter. Anything larger is apt to lose its shape. The braid from which it is made should be at least 1½" wide, but here again the beginning must be thinner than the rest of it. Make the base in the same way as described for the oval mat, i.e., with only the edges of the braid showing, and sew very firmly with strong twine. If light brown twine is used, it will hardly show. Bind the end of the braid very firmly with the twine and then coil it round on itself, going round and round until the base is the size required. The sides of the basket can be worked in the same way as the base, or you can make it in the same way as you made the shopping basket. The former method takes longer and requires a much longer braid but the result is certainly much more rigid and will, of course, wear better. When the basket is the correct height, taper off the braid as before and finish off the last row very gradually. A separate piece of braid should now be sewn all round the outside of the top, flat against the side of the basket, to form a decorative border. Bind the two ends and cut and sew them, so that they just touch. Make two short lengths of braid for the handles and sew in place in the same way as the handles of the shopping bag, being careful to put one handle over the join in the border.

A waste basket made on the same lines, although from a thinner braid, makes an attractive piece of furniture for a man's study.

Many people like raffia sandals for summer wear and a popular type is made on rope soles. Rush braid can be used very effectively as a substitute for the rope and it makes a softer foundation for the uppers. Be careful not to allow any stitches to appear on the underside, as they become worn through very quickly. A simple oval shape as described for the base of the shopping bag, is quite sufficient. If liked, a heel piece can be added at one end.

WEAVING WITH RUSHES

Rushes can be used singly for weaving and, whether the stakes are of reed or rush, the strokes used are exactly the same as those used in ordinary reed weaving—pairing, setting up, weaving, bordering, and so on. There is one important difference, however, between reed and rushes and this necessitates rather different methods of working with the two materials. This difference lies in the fact that whereas reed is 'springy' and will remain upright of its own accord, rushes are limp and 'floppy,' and have to be fixed in some way before you can weave them together.

A wooden, tin, or cardboard box with a lid makes a good foundation, and you must choose your box according to your own needs. The edges must be free from ridges or lips of any kind or you will find yourself unable to remove the foundation when the basket is finished. A rectangular wooden box makes a good foundation for a shopping basket, since it is convenient both as to shape and size. Small tacks or push pins are used for holding the rushes in place while the work is going on. If you cannot find a box of the right size and shape, however, you may have to make do with a cardboard one. This will be quite satisfactory

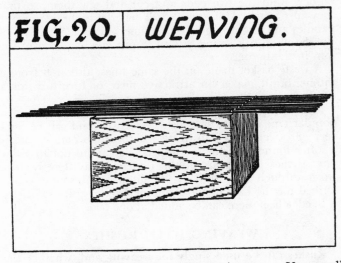

FIG. 20. | **WEAVING.**

provided the cardboard is thick and strong. Use small drawing pins for holding the rushes in place.

One of the long narrow sides of the box is used as a foundation for the base, the shorter narrow sides coming under the sides or gussets of the basket. Stand the box so that one of the long narrow sides is on top. Cut lengths of rush from the thick end. These rushes must be long enough to lie right along the box, plus enough over at each end to reach to the other side of the box. Lay the rushes evenly in a row along the box, placing thick and thin ends alternately, and allowing an equal amount to project at each side (see Fig. 20). Fix the rushes at one end with a tack, after flattening each one carefully between your finger and thumb. The exact number required depends on the width of the box and the thickness of the rushes you are using. Now cut another set of rushes. These are to be woven through the first at right angles, and they too should project for an equal distance at each side of the box. For an ordinary basket, this amount should be about 10″ or 12″. Weave each rush in turn through the first row, pushing each row as close to the previous row as possible, and securing with tacks after every half dozen or so, in order to keep the weaving straight. Alternate the thick and thin ends as you did before. As the basket has a woven pattern on each side you will need an uneven number of stakes for this. The ends may have an odd or even number. When the base is as closely woven as you can make it, remove the tacks and turn up the stakes for the sides. As you need an uneven number of stakes, add an extra one at one of the corners. Set the stakes by working two or three rows of ordinary pairing with the rushes, pressing each row well down.

Measure the depth you want your basket to be and calculate the approximate number of rows of weaving that will be required. Subtract nine from this number—this represents the number of rows required to weave the pattern in the centre of each side—and divide the remainder into two to find out how many rows must be worked before and after the pattern. Take care that the last row worked before the pattern, goes over the centre stake on each side. Work

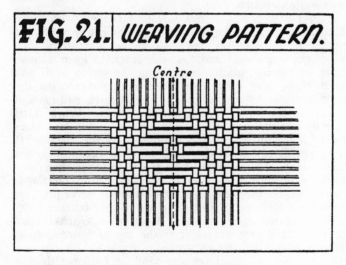

FIG. 21. WEAVING PATTERN.

Centre

the pattern as shown in Fig. 21, and then work the required number of rows, to complete the weaving. When it becomes necessary to join on a new piece, simply lay the new end over the old and work together for a few strokes.

Finish off the top of the basket by working two rows of pairing. The border—a three-rod plain border—is worked with the rush stakes, but in order to make it firmer, each stake is twisted once before every stroke. If this twisting is done evenly, it makes a most attractive border.

The handles of the basket may be made from twisted rushes or from a braid. In the latter case, simply sew into position at each side of the bag. A twisted handle is made as follows: Cut a length of rush about three times as long as you want your handles to be. Fold in half and pass one end through the side of the basket under the border and the top row of pairing. Twist each half separately to the right, then twist the two together. Continue in this way until the handle is long enough, then pass the ends through the border in opposite directions. Turn up the ends and bind very firmly with raffia or twine. Bind the other end of the handle to match.

Round baskets made on a box foundation should have their bases worked first, in exactly the same way as that of the plastic wire basket described above. Start with four rushes going one way and four the other, to form a cross. Work in pairing, gradually dividing the stakes until you are working over single ones. Add more stakes when the work is about 5″ across, choosing firm thick rushes, and pushing them well down into the weaving. Work until your base is the same size as the bottom of the box, then stand the tin on it and turn up the stakes for the side. If the stakes are rather far apart, add another stake in between each two, as the stakes must be closer together than they would be if more rigid material were being used. Over-and-under can be used for small baskets, but three-ply coil weaving or reverse coil will be found to give better results as the rows are closer together. If you wish to make your basket extra strong and rigid at the top or bottom, twist each stake once before each stroke.

Round baskets can have any kind of border although

the plainer borders are perhaps better than the braided ones, owing to the fact that a braided border needs to have the stakes absolutely even in size if it is to look really well.

A basket with sloping sides can be made, by using an ordinary flower pot as a base, provided it has no projecting edges.

Always allow woven rush baskets to dry thoroughly before you remove them from the foundation, as in this way the shape becomes properly set.

Since World War II synthetic rushes have become increasingly popular. These fibre rushes, made of twisted paper—3/32″, 5/32″ and 6/32″ in width—may be used in most cases for any project designed for the use of natural rushes.

COILED BASKETRY

WE come now to a most attractive branch of basketry and one which is pleasant and easy to do. Coiled basketry is one of the oldest and most universal of the crafts. Whether the vases and pots made by primitive man from long coils of clay rolled into shape and then coiled came first, or whether they were copied from the baskets already in existence, it is impossible to say. Traces of both have been found in excavations of primitive settlements. Whichever appeared first, however, it is certain that both go right back into the dawn of history.

Coiled basketry is almost always worked with some form of raffia, although the actual plant used may vary according to the locality. For the modern worker, raffia is the best material to use and, fortunately, it is plentiful and cheap. It can be obtained in natural and in various bright colours but whatever shade you prefer, your raffia must be of good quality, since only the raffia is seen in the finished product. It is worth while practising the various stitches, for they must be evenly and neatly worked, if the work is to look well.

The foundation used for making baskets in coiled work varies according to the degree of firmness required and the thickness you want your finished ridges to be. Reed is one of the most generally used materials, and you will find that the sizes numbered from four to seven are the most useful.

Thin reed does not give a firm enough fabric and the thicker sizes are too stiff to make for ease in handling. Beginners, however, will be well advised to start coiled work on a reed foundation as its smooth surface and evenness of thickness helps a great deal in keeping the work even.

For thicker coils, it is best to use thick string or rope, although it must be admitted that neither is quite so easy for the beginner to use. Raffia itself often forms the foundation for the coils and this has the advantage of enabling you to vary the thickness of the coil to suit yourself and the particular requirements of whatever you are making. It does have one disadvantage, however, and this is found in the fact that the length of the pieces of raffia is limited, and you are thus forced to make frequent joins.

The actual sewing of the coils is done with a blunt tapestry needle. This will pass through the space between the coils quite easily, but will not go through the reed. A needle with a sharp point should never be used, as it tends to split the raffia stitches, and so spoil the appearance of the work.

Various stitches are used for sewing the coils together and they all have one thing in common—they must be worked firmly and evenly, and they must cover the foundation completely. The size and thickness of the raffia used depends on the thickness of the foundation. Obviously, a thin piece of raffia wound round a thick piece of reed will look poor and mean, while a thick piece wound round thin reed will make the work look clumsy.

When working any kind of stitch, remember that the needle always goes from front to back, going away from and never towards the worker. You will notice from the illustrations that the stitches are worked from right to left, and most people will find this the most convenient way. There is no real reason, however, why you should not work from left to right, if you happen to find it easier.

Whatever stitch you use for the main part of a mat or basket, the centre of the coil is always worked in exactly the same way, although the method may vary a little, according to the material used from the foundation. Where

reed is used, the method is worked as follows. Shave the
end of the reed to a gradual point and dampen the first
few inches really well, coil the end round on itself as closely
as possible, working gently and gradually, so that the reed
does not split. Lay the end of the raffia along the top of
the reed and work over this end as well as the reed, until it
is covered. Work round and round into the centre hole,
which should be kept as small as possible until it is filled up
completely, as shown in Fig. 22. When you reach your starting point, you can start working whatever stitch you have
chosen.

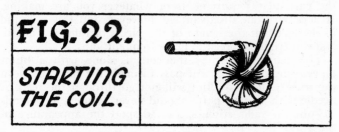

A raffia foundation is started in much the same way.
Take several strands of raffia and bind the ends together
very firmly, then coil them round and start the centre, as
before. Extra strands of raffia must be added as the work
proceeds until the coil is the thickness required. When
working over raffia in this way, pull the stitches very tightly
so that the raffia coil is as firm as possible.

When using string or rope, bind the end of the coil as
tightly as you can with strong thread in order to make the
end as thin as possible.

STITCHES

The easiest and one of the most popular of all stitches
in coiled basketry is known as Lazy Squaw or long and short
stitch. As its name implies, long and short stitch consists
of one long stitch going into the row beneath and one short
stitch going round the foundation only, as shown in Fig.
23. Pull the raffia firmly each time you go round the reed,

but not so tightly that you split it. Start the coil in the manner described above. When you reach your starting point, work a row of Lazy Squaw, putting each long stitch into the hole for the first round only. Wind the raffia once round the reed for each short stitch and, when the second round is reached, take the next long stitch into the space under a short stitch of the previous row.

When you need a new piece of raffia, simply lay the old end and the new one together along the top of the reed, and work over them until they are covered by your stitches.

A new piece of reed is joined on by shaving the end of each piece, old and new, laying them together and working over them as though they were one piece. If the fitting together is done properly, the join will be perfectly firm and will not show in the finished work.

As you progress, your work naturally gets bigger and you soon find it necessary to increase the number of stitches in each round. Increasing is done quite simply by putting two stitches into each space instead of one as seems necessary. There is no need to count the stitches between the increasing, unless you want these to form a definite pattern. You will get a better circle by spacing your increases so that you do not get them immediately above one another. Increasing is largely a matter of common sense and a little practice will soon enable you to judge when an increase is necessary. As all the stitches must look as though they radiate from the centre, you will know that an increase is required as soon as they begin to slope backwards.

There are several very attractive variations of Lazy Squaw stitch and they are all worked in much the same way. Peruvian coil (see Fig. 23) is one of the most popular. In its finished state, it appears to have lines radiating from the centre and these are worked as follows. Work a small coil of about two inches in diameter in Lazy Squaw stitch, being careful to finish the last round level with the beginning of the first one. On the next round, wind the raffia twice round the reed instead of once, before working the long stitch. This, of course, makes the long stitches a little farther apart. On the next round, wind the raffia three times round the reed before each long stitch and put the

FIG. 23. COILED BASKETRY.

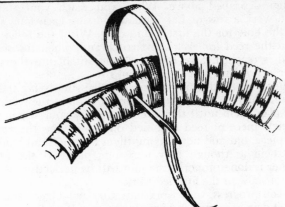

Lazy Squaw Stitch.

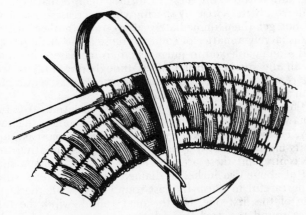

Peruvian Coil Stitch.

FIG. 24. | *STITCHES*

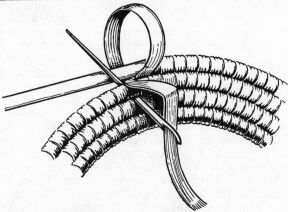

Figure Eight.

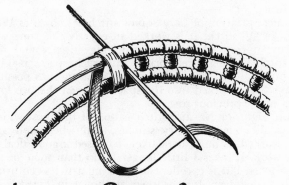

Lace Stitch or Mariposa.

long stitch immediately to the left of the long stitch on the previous row. Continue in this way, increasing the number of short stitches by one on each round for a little while. As the work grows you will probably find it sufficient to increase this number only on every second round, but this depends rather on the thickness of the raffia, and each worker must decide for herself, how often the increases are necessary on a particular piece of work. In actual practice, you will no doubt find that you will have to put in an extra row of long stitches. These should start midway between each pair of the original rows, thus adding extra ribs. The number of stitches made round the reed must never be so great as to make the work sloppy. Notice that, when working a flat coil such as a mat or the base of a basket, the lines all radiate from the centre. When they appear on the sides of a basket, they are slightly sloping, giving an attractive spiral effect. When working the sides of a basket, keep the number of short stitches more or less the same throughout.

The edge of a mat or basket worked in Peruvian coil should always be worked in Lazy Squaw stitch, to make it really firm.

Another variation of Lazy Squaw stitch is known as West African or 'V' stitch. It is worked in exactly the same way as Peruvian coil, except that two long stitches and one short stitch between are worked into each space, making a row of 'V's.' The rows must be kept as straight as possible and each 'V' is worked into the space between the two long stitches of the previous row.

Figure eight, or Navajo, stitch is one of the most widely used of all coiled basketry stitches, and when well and evenly worked, is most attractive. It is used a good deal in colour work. It takes a little longer to do than some of the other stitches, but is excellent for making articles requiring a really firm fabric. It is worked as shown in Fig. 24. As its name implies, the figure eight stitch is worked over two rows of reed in a figure eight. I have had to draw the stitch as if it were worked loosely, in order to make the method of working clear, but actually each half of the stitch is pulled tight as it is made, so that it looks rather as if the rows of reed have been bound closely with raffia and then joined invisibly. When working this stitch, keep the thickness of the raffia as even as possible, discarding each piece as soon as it becomes thin and ragged.

Lace stitch, or Mariposa stitch, is a stitch which gives a much lighter effect and is one which requires less reed for the foundation, as the knots hold the rows a little way apart. It is worked as shown in Fig. 24. It is not generally used on a thick foundation, as the distance between the reeds is determined by the thickness of the knots and, as these are never very large, they do not show up well when the coil is a great deal wider than the space between the rows.

The Mariposa is used to add interest and lightness to a piece of work. It looks well when used in conjunction with the figure eight stitch. A set of table mats may be worked in alternate bands of Mariposa and the Lazy Squaw stitch. When two or more stitches are used in one piece of work, it is better to keep the article to one colour. Conversely, when several colours are used, the work is in better taste if only one stitch is used.

FINISHING OFF

The finishing off of an article in coiled basketry is very important, since it must be secure and at the same time as unobtrusive as possible. For a reed foundation, simply shave off the end very gradually and go on working until the foundation is completely covered. The raffia is fastened off neatly, by working under and over alternate rows of the coils and cutting off the end inside. A raffia coil is finished off by gradually lessening the number of strands in the foundation. Do not cut off the ends all in the same place, as this makes too abrupt an ending. String on rope should be untwisted for a few inches, and the strands cut off a few at a time.

SHAPING A BASKET

So far, we have considered the work 'in the flat' as it were, but it must be borne in mind that most coiled basketry is devoted to the making of baskets or bows. The shaping of such articles is most important from the point of view of both appearance and usefulness. Getting a good shape is not difficult but it needs a good deal of practice, especially in getting both sides of a basket to match. I know of no mechanical method of shaping a basket, so that you have to work more or less 'by eye.' When you want the sides of a basket to slope outwards, place each succeeding row of reed a little farther out than the one before. When you want it to slope inwards, simply reverse the procedure and place the reed a little further in. There are endless variations to be made in the shape of coiled baskets, and it is probable that no two baskets are ever exactly alike. It is wise, however, to decide on the shape of your basket before you begin to work the sides, and not simply make it up as you go along. A rough sketch will help you to keep in mind the shape you are aiming at.

Square or oblong baskets are not usually made in coiled basketry. Oval ones, though not so usual as round ones, are attractive and easy to make. Decide how long you want the base of your basket to be. Measure about two-fifths of this length along the reed. Dampen the reed very well, squeeze with pliers and bend the reed round at this point, so that it forms a hairpin shape, sew the two sides of this hairpin together, using the figure eight stitch. Turn the reed round at the end of this row and work down the opposite side of the first row. Continue working round and round, until the base is the correct size. Work the sides exactly as you would for a round basket. An oval fruit basket worked in this way is attractive and useful. Work the base as just described, using figure eight stitch to make sure that the base is perfectly rigid. Work the sides so that they slope outwards, using one or two of the other stitches. A band of Mariposa with a border of figure eight stitch would look pretty. Use a medium width reed for the foundation and keep the raffia fairly thick in order to make the knots in the Mariposa show up well and keep the coils the proper distance apart.

MAKING A SET OF TABLE MATS

Table mats in coiled basketry wear better, I think, than

almost any other kind, providing that they are well made in the first place. They give you practice in working the stitches, without the bother of shaping sides. A medium sized reed should be used for the foundation of the coils. Raffia, as a foundation, is not so good, as it is not so easy to get a perfectly flat surface—a very necessary quality in dinner mats. Dampen the reed and start the coil as described above. Work in Lazy Squaw stitch, increasing as required until the work measures about 4½" across. This gives a good solid centre on which the plate can rest. Now work a band of Mariposa about 3" wide, and another band of Lazy Squaw about 1" wide, to finish off the edge. This will give you a mat about 11" in diameter, but, of course, the sizes you can make, and the arrangement of the bands, can be varied indefinitely to suit your own particular needs and tastes. When making large mats, it is a good idea to work alternate narrower bands of the Mariposa and any other stitch you may wish to use, as too much Mariposa is apt to make the mat rather too flexible.

An extremely attractive set of mats can be made by working with two colours, using the figure eight stitch. Work about 4" in one colour, then work all the succeeding rounds in two colours, as follows. Work either one-third or one-sixth of a round in the contrasting colour, the next third or sixth in the original colour, and so on for all succeeding rounds.

TUMBLER HOLDER

This is a most useful little article in which to put a tumbler containing a beverage. It must fit the tumbler really closely, so that even if you pick up the tumbler itself, the holder will remain in place. The size of the holder depends on the particular tumbler you wish to provide it for, but 3" high by about 2¼" across the base would fit a more or less standard size in tumblers. Make a flat coil exactly as described for the mats, working until it is just large enough to fit the base of the tumbler. Now, instead of stitching the next row of reed on top of the previous row, put it level with it, away from you and inside the work, and work over it as before. Continue in the same way, keeping the sides almost but not quite straight. The usual tendency in working the sides is to make them slope out too much, so try the holder on the tumbler at frequent intervals, to make sure that it is a really good fit. The sides can be worked in any stitch you like, but the holder should have a border of the figure eight or Lazy Squaw stitch. A coloured motif worked into each side would look well but, as the article is not very large, should be kept small and neat.

LIDDED BASKETS

Workbaskets made in coiled basketry are always attractive and, if well made, will last for a long time. They can be of almost any shape you like, although from the point of view of the person who is going to use such a basket, they are best if they are simple in shape with a wide top. Workbaskets should always be padded and lined when they are finished, preferably with some kind of smooth-surfaced material. Many people prefer such a basket to have a lid, although they can be finished with a gathered top, as described in a previous chapter. Lids are made in exactly the same way as the base, except that they are slightly shaped during the working. A lid with sloping sides is not only more attractive to look at, but will remain in place better. Pad and line the lid to match the rest of the basket. Join the lid to the basket with a hinge made from several long stitches worked in raffia, and fasten with a button and a buttonhole loop. I have seen most attractive workbaskets made in this way, using a raffia base, and either Peruvian coil or West African stitch. The lids were finished with a spray of embroidery worked in coloured raffia. Such a basket could be made at home for the price of the raffia and several hours' work, but would be expensive if bought in a shop.

HANDLES

WHEN we come to the making of shopping baskets, we are
at once confronted with the problem of making a handle.
The handle of a basket is an important feature for not
only must it be attractive and in keeping with the style of
the basket, but it must be strong and easy to hold.

There are several ways of making handles on coiled
baskets, the type you choose depending on the size and
shape of your basket. Handles made 'all in one' with the
basket are to be preferred for larger baskets, as they are
stronger, and not so likely to wear out the stitches joining
them to the main part but, for small baskets, handles may
be worked first and sewn on afterwards. A thick braid made
from raffia makes an attractive handle that is quick to
work. Another method is to decide on the length you want
your handle to be and to stitch several lengths of reed
together to make it. Bend the well-damped reed round, as
described for the oval base, and work round and round
until the handle is the width you want. Sew it very firmly
indeed to the basket. If the handle is placed inside, the
stitches on the outside may be hidden by an embroidered
flower. One advantage these handles have over those worked
on to the basket is that they can be removed and replaced
more easily and this is a good thing, as the handle is often
the part that wears out first.

A handle made 'all in one' with the basket is worked as
follows. Finish off the top of the basket in the usual way.

Mark two points exactly opposite to one another on the top edge, by slipping a piece of raffia through. Shave the ends of a piece of reed and, starting at a point midway between the two marks, work over the reed using the figure eight stitch, until you come to a point about 2″ from the first marked point. Now take the reed over to the other side and join it to the top of the basket again about 2″ from the first mark. Go on working for three or four rounds, according to the thickness of the reed and the width you want your finished handle to be. Fasten off the end just over the place where you began. This completes the first half of the handle. Turn the basket round and work the second half in the same way, joining the first row of this to the first row of the first half. The join should start and finish about three inches or so above the edge of the basket, leaving an open triangle at each end of the handle. If preferred, of course, the handle can be joined along its entire length, in which case the first row of reed must be taken right up to the central mark and then taken over the basket at right angles to the top edge. When working a handle of this type, be very careful to see that the centre of the handle on one side is exactly opposite to the centre on the other side, so that the basket will be properly balanced.

COLOURED WORK

The American Indians and the natives of parts of Africa make lovely coiled baskets into which they work intricate designs in several colours. Many of these designs are traditional and symbolical, and are peculiar to a particular tribe or family.

Colour work in coiled basketry is conditioned by the peculiar properties of this type of work. These special points must be borne in mind when coloured patterns are being planned. In the first place, a flat round piece of coiled basketry is not a true circle. Careful finishing off may make a mat appear to be perfectly round, but as soon as you try to introduce a pattern, particularly one based on a circle, you find that this is an illusion and that, in fact, the mat is a spiral.

It is owing to this fact that broken designs work out better than continuous ones. If you want to introduce a simple coloured stripe, for instance, you will find that the two ends do not join up properly, for when you reach the end of the round you will find that this end will be a step above the beginning. A better way would be to plan your pattern in the form of separate motifs, arranging it so that the join in each row comes in between two of them. Two of the motifs, of course, will not be exactly level, but this will not be noticeable in the finished work, particularly if it appears on the sides of a basket.

Designs used in coiled basketry should always be sketched before they are incorporated into a basket. Measure the circumference of the base of your basket, and draw a rectangle on a piece of plain paper, with this length as the length of one side. The other side should be the same length as the height you want your basket to be. The worked base will give you an idea of how many rows there will be in the sides, so divide up your rectangle by drawing parallel horizontal lines across it. The number of

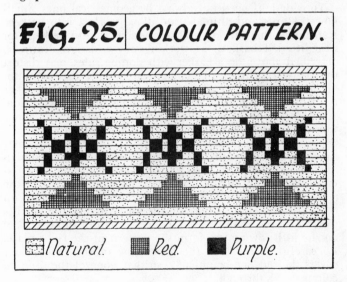

FIG. 25. COLOUR PATTERN.

▦ Natural. ▨ Red. ■ Purple.

spaces so formed will correspond with the number of rows you propose to put into the sides of the basket. Now draw a simple geometrical design on your paper. Fig. 25 shows a simple pattern that is well within the scope of even a beginner. You will notice that in the diagram the end motifs (which will be next to one another when the design is worked on a circular basket), appear to be exactly level. In the finished work, one motif will appear to be one row higher than the other, but this need not worry you as it will not be very noticeable.

You will notice that I have not mentioned the number of stitches in each section. This is because raffia varies so much in its thickness that you can never be sure that say, twelve stitches in one part of the row will cover exactly the same amount of reed as twelve stitches in another part. The patterns are, therefore, worked out by measurement—one inch of red say, then two of natural and one of blue. Use a tape measure to check your measurements, it is more accurate than a ruler on curved articles, and put pencil marks on the row beneath to act as guides.

Your designs need not always be geometrical ones. Small flowers, birds and animals can all be worked into baskets. Remember that any naturalistic designs should be kept for straight-sided baskets, as working out a design drawn as described above, on a basket with sloping sides, may distort the pattern a little. In geometrical designs this does not matter and indeed often adds to its attractiveness, but other types of pattern may be spoiled by the inevitable distortion.

There is one very important thing to remember about working colour designs, especially when you are using a figure eight stitch. Always start the pattern one row later than appears on your chart. Thus, supposing your design consists of four plain rows with the first row of a coloured motif appearing on the fifth row, you would not start the new colour until you arrived at the appropriate place on the sixth row. This is because the lower half of the stitches worked on the sixth row cover the top half of those worked on the fifth row and so form the pattern in the right place. Be careful to see that the lower row of the new colour covers the old one completely, so that none of the original colour shows through.

When you reach the end of the motif, you will find that you will appear to have one row too many, but this will be put right when you work the next row, since the lower halves of the stitches in the main colour will cover up the top halves of those in the contrasting colour.

When working out a design for a flat mat, draw a circle on a piece of plain paper and fill it with evenly-spaced concentric circles, making the spaces between the lines represent the number of rows you propose to work. Draw one of the radius of the outer circle and make this line represent the beginnings of the rows. Try to arrange your pattern so that this join always comes in the part of the row worked in the main or background colour.

Starting on a new colour is done in exactly the same way as starting on a new piece of the same colour. Where only a few stitches in each colour are required, it is quite permissible to use both colours at once, the one not actually needed being taken along the top of the reed while you work over it with the other.

As a general rule, the simpler the decoration, the more effective it is. Good workmanship will always be attractive while no amount of decoration added afterwards will conceal faults in the actual working of the stitches.

If some kind of decoration does seem to be called for, use large simple designs in embroidered raffia. Any of the baskets described above may be finished, if you wish, with a coat of clear varnish. This will help to prevent fraying when the basket is in use and will make the work easier to clean.

A LAUNDRY BASKET

A large and roomy linen basket is an asset to any bathroom or bedroom, although some found in the shops are often extremely expensive. It is possible, however, to make a most attractive and useful one from raffia. A really thick coil of raffia should be used for the foundation, as reed of the thickness needed would be far too difficult to work. The finished ridges should be at least an inch wide. Although this is a large piece of work, it should not take a great deal longer to do than a smaller and finer basket, since it takes no longer to work an inch of stitches over a thick coil than it does over a thin one. Use the raffia in pieces that are as wide as possible. Any thin pieces can be used up in the foundation coil. Always thread the raffia into the needle widest end first, as this prevents fraying and splitting.

Start the basket by making a fairly thin coil, and sewing it very firmly. Work the base in figure eight stitch, keeping it perfectly flat. Add more strands of raffia to the foundation as the circle grows, until you have enough to make each coil at least an inch deep. When the base measures about 16" across, start working the sides. Work these in Peruvian coil, and keep them absolutely perpendicular. Work until the sides are about 27" high, then work a final row very firmly in a figure eight or Lazy Squaw stitch. Fasten off the last coil gradually, making sure that the top of the basket is perfectly level.

Start the lid just as you did the base, but when it is about 3" across, change to Peruvian coil, and work so that the sides slope slightly. When the lid is just big enough to fit on to the top of the basket, fasten off the coil. Now start a new one, putting it at right angles to the edge of the lid and working round for two rows. Fasten off gradually so that the rim is level all the way round. Start another coil, this time above the rim, joining it to the last row of the sloping part, so that you have a projecting rim all round on top of the part which fits into the basket.

Make a circular handle for the top of the lid by forming several strands of raffia into a circle about 2½" across, and binding very tightly with a piece of damp smooth raffia. An alternative method would be to work over the strands in buttonhole stitch. A very large curtain ring could also be used as a foundation. Whichever method you choose, be careful to sew the ring very firmly to the centre of the lid as it will no doubt get a lot of hard wear.

A similar basket, though very much smaller, could serve as a waste basket, though it would not, of course, require a lid. Either basket would look well decorated with flat stitches forming flowers and leaves, and worked in coloured raffia. Do not make these stitches too large, as they are apt to become frayed and ragged.

An extremely hard wearing and attractive rug or mat can be made from raffia, using the usual coiled basketry stitches. Figure eight is perhaps the most suitable, as this ensures that each row of the foundation is covered twice. Thick rope can be used for the foundation, and can be used straight from the hank in which it is bought, thus obviating the necessity for making joinings while the work is in progress.

A USEFUL BREAD BASKET

A little further back, I mentioned that coiled basketry is always spiral in character and not truly circular. There is, however, one type of coiled basketry which comes into the same category as the baskets we have already considered, and which is not spiral. I have left it until last, because it is a little more difficult than the more ordinary type, since it demands great neatness and accuracy if it is to be a success.

Openwork baskets, consisting of carefully spaced coils separated by a form of Mariposa, are useful for bread or fruit baskets and, being open, they take the minimum of reed.

Make a centre measuring about 2″ across in ordinary coiled work, using Mariposa with raffia on a medium reed. Shave off the end and fasten off in the usual way. Divide the circumference of the centre into eight, placing pencil marks to indicate the divisions.

The base of the basket is made from six concentric circles, each about ½″ larger in diameter than the one before. Measure each one as you need it, cutting each piece of reed about 2″ longer than the circumference of the circle required. Shave off the ends and fit one over the other to make a neat join. A piece of raffia tied around the join will hold it in place while you are working, and can be removed when you are ready to cover this part of the circle.

Fit the circle over the centre of the basket, holding it in place with temporary ties. Now take a piece of very thin flat wrapping reed, fine willow skein or raffia, and start wrapping the circle at a point between the ties. When you reach a marked spot, make a lace stitch into the foundation circle, then go on winding until you reach the next pencil mark. Remove each tie and the binding round the join as you come to it. When you reach the end of the circle, work the last few turns loosely, tuck the end under them and pull them tight, cutting the end off close.

Make the next circle and tie in place, as before. Work round the circle as in the previous row, but this time make two lace stitches at each marked place, putting one on each side of the knot in the previous row. Fasten this row off and make the next circle. The third circle has three knotted stitches in each group and the fourth has four. When you come to the fifth and sixth rows, decrease the number of knotted stitches, so that you will have three and two respectively. This completes the base of the basket, and you are now ready for the sides.

Make each circle just as for the base, but lessen the difference in circumference between. Each circle should be just big enough to rest on the outer edge of the previous row without actually slipping over, so that when all the circles are in place, the sides will be sloping. On the first round of the sides, work sixteen knot stitches. One stitch is worked between each two of the previous round, thus completing the eight diamond shapes in the base, and another is worked between each of these and forms the starting point of one of the eight diamond shapes in the sides. Add four more rounds, increasing the number of stitches in these diamonds until you have five stitches in each group. On the next two rounds, decrease the knot stitches to four and three. On the next round work two knot stitches in each group and add an extra knot stitch on all the spaces between the groups. On the final round, work one knot stitch over each group, and two (one on either side) over the single knot stitches.

The border of the basket consists of two rows of reed placed one outside the other and fitting closely together. Work the rim closely and firmly in lace stitch, and fasten off very securely.

PLASTIC BASKETRY

We do not, as a rule, associate coiled basketry with plastic materials, but there is no real reason why we should not apply the methods and designs used in the traditional way with reed, to articles made from the latest addition to our available materials.

We have already mentioned plastic wire as being suitable for use in making woven baskets, and this can be used just as well for the foundation of coiled work. Spools of plastic thread in a good selection of colours can be obtained, and this thread is used in exactly the same way as raffia. You will probably find that you need to increase your stitches a little more frequently when using plastic products but this is a matter that is easily adjusted as you work. Medium and thick wire should be used for the foundation. The stitches used for coiled basketry are quite suitable for working with plastic products. Lazy Squaw and Mariposa stitch are perhaps more effective and easier to work than figure eight stitch, although this may be used quite successfully too.

The way in which the coil begins varies a little from the way in which the coils made with reed or raffia start. Bind the end of the wire firmly for about 1½″ with the plastic, bend it round to form a small ring and go on working in the stitch you have chosen.

A plastic soap dish in coiled basketry makes a useful and attractive little addition to bathroom or kitchen, and is something that can only be made from non-porous material such as plastic. Bend your narrow plastic wire round into a hairpin shape, so that the short end measures about 2¼″. Fasten the two sides together, using figure eight stitch, then work round and round using lace stitch. When the base measures about 4½″ long, start the sides, making them quite straight and about an inch deep.

Articles made from plastic materials can be washed quite easily and, if made in well chosen colours, are very attractive.

RAFFIA WORK

So far, we have mentioned raffia quite frequently but have not, as yet, considered it as a material in its own right. It can, however be used for making all kinds of bags, baskets and other things, without any other material being needed.

Raffia can be braided, wound or woven. Raffia braids make most attractive bags, waste baskets, sandals and so on, and articles made in this way are very cheap.

It is not necessary to buy the most expensive kinds of raffia for making raffia braids, although if you want the coloured variety, you will naturally have to pay more for it.

Always dampen your bundle of raffia before braiding it, as this makes the work smoother and easier. The number of strands you put in your braid depends on the article you want to make and the way in which you intend to use your material. Tie the ends of the raffia together and hang from a convenient hook or nail. As in the case of making braids from rushes, you will find it easier to work out-of-doors. When the braid becomes too long to handle easily, remove it from the hook, loop a piece of string round it, just above the part you have reached, and go on working as before. As the raffia becomes used up you must add new strands to keep the braid of an even thickness. Lay the new end over the old one, work together for a few turns, then leave the old end inside the braid. Try not to get a lot of joins in the same place as this weakens the braid as well as making it a little uneven. Any ends that refuse to lie smoothly in the work can be snipped off afterwards.

When braiding the raffia, you will find that you get a better result if you make each turn short and tight. The way in which the raffia is braided makes a great deal of difference to the finished work, for a loosely worked braid will never make a firm fabric, however closely you sew the rows together.

Braided raffia is often used in conjunction with reed for making the sides of baskets. I have already dealt with this branch of reedwork, and it is sufficient to say here that braids used in this way should be narrow, being never more, and preferably less, than ½″ wide. As a rule, over-and-under is used when they are woven into the basket, as the braids are too thick for it to be practicable to use any other stroke. It is a good idea to work a row of pairing or three-ply coil at intervals to help to keep the work rigid.

When we come to articles made by sewing the braids together, our scope is considerably enlarged. The method is similar to that used in making articles from braided rush but, as the raffia is altogether thinner and lighter than the rush, smaller and daintier things can be made from it.

SHOPPING BAGS

There are several types of shopping bags which look well when they are made from raffia braids. One of the most attractive is the sort made by sewing two flat circles together with a gusset between. The thicker the braid, the quicker the work will be done, but be careful not to make your braid too thick or the work will be clumsy.

Bind the end of the braid very firmly with a strip of raffia, then coil it round on itself, sewing each round firmly to the one before, until the work is about 12″ across. Make the second side in exactly the same way. Now measure two-thirds of the way round the circle. Take a new piece of braid, bind the end, and fold it as far from the end as the measurement you have just made. Sew the two sides together, then work round and round until you have made a long oval piece about 4″ wide. Sew this strip between the two circles to form the gusset. It is a good idea to finish off the bag by sewing a circle, made from a thinner braid in a contrasting colour, all round each side of the bag. If preferred, too, the bag can be decorated with a spray of flowers embroidered in raffia.

The handles are made from a thicker braid and may be sewn inside or outside the bag, according to the preference of the worker. These bags wear very well and, being the same on both sides, require no lining.

Two-colour work is extremely effective when used for work of this kind, but if you want to put two colours into one braid, you will find that it is better to use a braid made from four strands rather than one made from three. Braiding with four strands is one of those things that everybody knows how to do until he or she comes to it. It is, however, very simple being based on ordinary under-and-over weaving. The same method is used for braids containing any number of strands.

The way in which you arrange your strands at the beginning, makes a difference to the pattern of your braid. If you arrange your colours alternately say, natural, blue, natural, blue, you will get a braid containing alternate blue and natural stripes. If you arrange your strands in two groups with two natural and two blue side by side, you will get a zig-zag effect. Whichever arrangement of colours you prefer, the method of working is the same. Tie your strands together in the usual way and arrange the colours in the correct order. Take the right hand strand and weave it over, under and over the other three, leaving it on the right hand side. Now take the right hand strand again—this was the second from the right when you began—and weave it across in the same way. Continue in this way, always starting on the right until the braid is as long as you want it, joining in new strands as you require them.

SHOPPING BAG IN THREE COLOURS

When you require a rather larger bag, you will find that one made from an oval is better than one made from two circles, since it is firmer and holds more. Here are instructions for making such a bag in natural, orange and brown raffia. Any other colours could be used just as effectively. Start by making a length of half-inch braid in natural raffia. Measure fifteen inches from one end and fold at this point. Work round and round on this first 15″ as a foundation, until your oval measures about 6″ or 7″ across. Reduce the width of the braid as you get near to the end, tuck the bound end under the last row and fasten off firmly. Make a braid with four strands, using two of brown and two of orange. Sew this round and round the centre of the bag until you have worked a border about 3″ wide. Finally, make a three-braid in brown, and sew round the outside of the oval to make a 2″ border. Make an oval gusset for each side, each about 4″ wide and deep enough to fit between the two halves of the oval when it is folded. Sew the gusset in place, then make two braids from the brown raffia for the handles.

A handbag made on the same lines, using much finer braids, is attractive when used with summer dresses. The gusset on such a bag should be continued right round and have a zip-fastened opening in the centre and arranged across the top. The handle can be made from two braids sewn together and lined with upholstery braid to prevent stretching, or it can be made from a plastic or leather belt.

Handbags of the envelope type, too, can be made from braided raffia but the braids must be very firm and tight and the bag should be well-stiffened with cardboard or buckram. A large wooden bead or button makes an appropriate fastening.

Raffia braids can be used to make rugs which will give quite a satisfactory amount of wear. The method used is exactly the same as that used for making rush mats, and needs no repetition here. Raffia braid is, I think, easier and cleaner to handle than that made from rushes and you have a much wider choice of colours than you will find in rushes.

Another advantage that raffia has over rush is that, being much thinner, it can be used for making a much larger variety of articles. Tiny braids made from three single strands can be used to make dress ornaments while those only a little thicker can be used for hats and sandals by the usual method of sewing the braids together in rows, to get the required shape.

Table mats in several colours can be made from raffia braids and they look most attractive and wear well if two oval or circular pieces are made for each mat. These are sewn together round the edge, with a piece of stiff cardboard sandwiched between.

RAFFIA WINDING

Another method of making bags which is very popular at the moment, partly I think because it is so simple that a child can do it, is to cover small cardboard circles with raffia and sew them together to the shape required. Each circle should not be more than 2″ across—say, the size of a silver dollar—and should have a hole about ½″ in diameter, in the centre. Cover each circle with buttonhole stitch, being careful to see that no cardboard shows through, lay them flat on the table in the pattern you prefer and sew them firmly together where they touch. Finish with a handle of braided or twisted raffia or rush.

Other articles, such as dinner mats, desk blotters, etc., can be made in the same way. This sort of work gives one a lot of scope for working out effective patterns and colour schemes, and is a good way of using up all those odd lengths of raffia which seem to accumulate so quickly.

RAFFIA WEAVING

Although raffia weaving does not, strictly speaking, come under the heading of basketwork, it has much in common with other methods of making bags and baskets. It is not particularly suitable for use in weaving the sides of reed baskets, since the stakes have to be very close together if the result is to be firm enough to be of any practical use, but used on a warp strung on a cardboard loom and made of thin string, raffia weaving can be very effective. Suitably shaped looms for making shopping bags, coasters and slippers can now be bought, or you can make your own. The raffia is simply woven in and out in the ordinary under and over fashion, common to all weaving.

CHAPTER IX

SEATING STOOLS WITH HONG KONG GRASS

ONE very useful and decorative type of work which comes under the heading of basketry—although it is not actually concerned with the making of baskets—is that of seating stools or chairs with Hong Kong grass, a most delightful material to use. In the form in which it comes to us, it is a continuous twisted rope. In colour, it is a pleasant shade of beige or it can be obtained in a good variety of shades such as green, brown, rust, and so on. A combination made of two colours twisted together can also be bought. The price varies a little according to where you buy it, and quantities available are subject to world conditions as they affect imported products.

The usual purpose for which Hong Kong grass is used is for the making of stool and chair seats although, as I have mentioned earlier, it can also be used for making baskets in conjunction with reed or willow. It has the merit of being pliable to handle and is evenly and smoothly twisted in lengths that are as long as anyone is likely to need. Incidentally, a good substitute for this grass is seating cord, which can also be obtained in natural shade and colours. It is more expensive than the grass, but as it is a little finer than the grass you would probably get more to the pound. A stool seated with the cord would take a little longer to do but the finished effect is smoother and finer.

A stool measuring say, about 13″ square, would require about a pound of the grass or seating cord, although if you wish to introduce a contrasting colour, you may find you have to buy a little more.

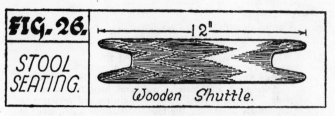

FIG. 26.

STOOL SEATING.

|← 12″ →|

Wooden Shuttle.

There are one or two special tools which you will need if you wish to make a seat with either cord or Hong Kong grass, but they are neither elaborate nor expensive. You may use a shuttle which you can make yourself as shown in Fig. 26, though many workers prefer to do the work with their hands. A piece of flat plywood can be used, although strong cardboard will serve the purpose just as well, except that it will need renewing sooner. If you intend to make a woven seat, you will also need a special long needle known as a seating needle, which costs very little. A piece of dowelling rod ½″ in diameter is needed for this work, and it should be long enough to go right across the stool.

Wooden stool frames of all types are on the market, and you should have no difficulty in getting just the size and shape you want. A small stool measuring say, 12″ x 10½″ x 9″ can be obtained for a couple of dollars with the larger ones costing more in proportion to their size. If you are by way of being a carpenter you can, of course, make your own stool frame, and this will enable you to provide yourself with a frame which exactly suits your own taste. Separate legs can be bought from some woodworker's shops and with the addition of four straight pieces of wood for the top and another four to act as stretchers, can be made into suitable frames. Before making a stool frame, it is a good idea to examine one or two ready-made ones, as these are specially designed to make the working of the top easy.

The stool must be stained, polished or enamelled before the seating is begun. Make sure that the surface is perfectly smooth before you begin. The stool frames sold in the shops are made from several types of wood, which can be finished in any one of the ways mentioned above.

There are two methods of making the stool tops. The first is the one in which the necessary number of strands is laid across the stool to form a warp, with the rest of the grass woven into it at right angles to form a weft. This method is, I think, a little easier for the beginner, and it does give more scope for working patterns of various kinds. As against this, it is not suitable for larger stools as it is inclined to sag, and it cannot be used for seating chairs, unless the front and back rails are exactly the same width.

The second method is one which is built up by working round the corners and over the frames. This gives an exceedingly strong seat, for it has three layers of the grass in it, and the slight hollow produced in the centre certainly makes for comfort in sitting on it. It does not give many opportunities for introducing patterns, although you can use one or more colours for putting in contrasting stripes.

Having made and prepared your stool, you are ready to begin weaving the top. First of all mark the centre of each top piece or rail, and, while working remember that you must have an equal number of strands on each side of each mark. Wind about twenty yards or so of the grass on your shuttle, if you are using one. Tie a knot in the end and tack it firmly through the knot to the frame just inside the left front corner. Lay the dowel rod across the centre of the frame so that, as you take the strand across from the front to the back, it will have to go over the rod. This will help to keep your rows even in tension and, at the same time, enable you to make them loose enough for the second row to be woven in and out easily.

Bring the strand up, inside the front rail, wind it twice round the rail close to the leg and take it right across to the back rail, going underneath the stool. Wind it twice round the back rail, then bring it back to the front on the top side. Now wind it smoothly and evenly right over the frame for three more turns, so that you have four strands lying neatly side by side. Be very careful not to allow them to cross over one another, particularly on the underside. Take two more turns round the front rail, take the grass underneath to the back rail, go twice round this rail and back to the front on the top side. Continue in this way

right across the frame, ending with two turns round each
rail to match the first two. There are, of course, many variations of this pattern. For instance, you could make each
row consist of two or three rows with only one turn
between. Whichever pattern you choose for the first side,
however, must be repeated when you work the second side
into it.

The stool is now ready for the second row or weft. Unwind the strands from the shuttle as this is too thick to go
through the rows you have already worked. Take out the
rod over which you have been working, as it will not be
required any longer.

Since you started your first layer at the front left hand
corner, you will have finished it at the back right hand
corner. Take it out to the right and under the right hand
rail, winding it twice round this rail close to the top of the
leg. Bring it down inside, turn the stool over and take it
across the underneath, going under the centre group of
four only. Turn the stool right side up, go twice round the
left hand rail, then go back to the right hand side across the
top, weaving under one group of four rows and over the
next. Take three more turns round the stool, going under
and over the same groups as the first row. Take two more
turns round the right hand rail, turn the stool over and
take the grass under one group of four rows about halfway
between the rail and the centre group on each side. This
method is followed for the whole of the underside, alternate groups of four going under the one group and the
same two groups on alternate rows. Continue in the same
way until the whole of the stool is covered. Finish off by
tying a knot in the end and tacking it to the inside of the
frame. The work is not very quick but can be speeded up
by using a weaving needle. A flat wooden rod used after
the manner of a needle is also a help, as it can be turned
so that it makes a passage through the rows of weaving
through which the needle can be passed easily. Keep your
strands as even in tension as possible as you work. If you
should have to lay it aside before the weaving is complete,
wind the Hong Kong grass very tightly round one of the
legs.

Simple weaving, such as I have just described, always

looks well, but if you want a more closely woven seat, you should leave out one of the turns round the rails. Two rows in each group will also give you a closer weave, while a closer weave still can be obtained by using a diagonal or herringbone weaving. Indeed, the possibilities are endless.

Introduction of Hong Kong grass in a contrasting colour considerably widens our scope where variation in pattern is concerned. Where coloured stripes are used, it is better to keep the actual weaving simple in character, or you may find that the finished article is fussy and over-elaborate. You will find many different arrangements of stripes being used in this sort of work. Remember to calculate the number of rows required before you begin, so that you can make a rough sketch of the design you propose to use.

When your strand has to be joined, as it will when you wish to introduce another colour, tie the ends in a reef knot on the underside, and tuck them neatly between the two rows of weaving.

The second method, which I have already mentioned, is a little more difficult to keep even, but if you work carefully you should be able to manage it quite successfully. Prepare your stool in the usual way and wind the grass on to a shuttle. Tie a knot in the end, and tack it firmly to the stool on the inside of the back rail, close to the leg on the right hand side. Take it over the back rail, down the back and up on the inside. Take it out to the right, over the right hand rail and back to the inside again. Take it over the left hand rail, going right across the stool and back to the inside. Now take it over the back rail, going over the grass at the same time. Bring it back to the inside, to the front and over the left hand rail. Bring it up inside and take it out to the right and over the right hand rail. Bring it up inside, over the front rail and up inside again. Take it to the back, over the back rail by the side of the first turn and back inside again. You are now back where you started, and must continue going round the stool in exactly the same way until the whole of the inside space is filled. You will notice that as the work grows, each turn is taken over the long strands going from side to side, as well as over the rail (Fig. 27).

Try to keep your tension as even as possible, as this not

only makes the work look better, it helps it to wear better, too. Be careful to see that the lines cross each other at right angles, otherwise you may find that the diagonal lines are wavy instead of straight. It is advisable to try to finish your stool top without stopping, but if you do have to put it on one side before it is completed, wind the material

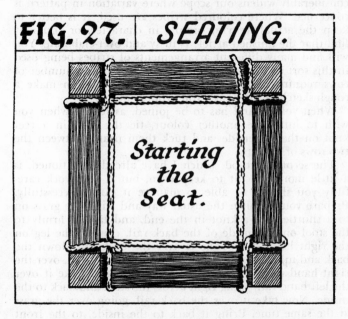

FIG. 27. | SEATING.

Starting
the
Seat.

very firmly round one of the legs, as it is very difficult to tighten up the weaving once it has been allowed to become slack.

As you work, you will naturally find that the hole in the centre will gradually get smaller until you will have to discard the shuttle and wind the material into a small hank. Finally, you will have to unwind this and simply pull the end through each time. When the hole is completely filled, wind the end of the material in and out of the underneath rows a few times and tie so that it cannot come undone.

If you wish to make an oblong stool by this method, you will obviously finish the short sides before the long ones are complete. In this case, you simply fill up the remaining space by working backwards and forwards over the side rails in the form of a figure eight.

Hong Kong grass is not particularly easy to work, as it has to be worked tightly, so be careful not to do too much at once. A pair of gloves is a help in grasping the material and will prevent your hands from becoming sore.

This method of seating need not be confined to stools, for chairs can be re-seated in the same way. Start the material exactly as you would for a stool, and work in exactly the same way. You may find that the back of the seat will become filled up first, if it is narrower than the front, but this can be remedied by taking an extra turn round the front rail every so often, and by allowing the front rows to be a little further apart than the back ones. Be careful to arrange these rows evenly, so that they are not close together on one side of the front rail, and too far apart on the other.

This type of seat seems to go particularly well with ladder-back chairs. You will often find these seats worked with rush instead of with grass, and if you are prepared to go to a little extra trouble you will find that you can use the rushes quite easily. Prepare the rushes in the usual way by soaking them, and cut off all the thin ends. Rushes are, of course, not continuous and must be joined. Lay one end over the other, and go on working. When the seat is finished, the ends can be tucked neatly under the top or bottom layer. It is not advisable to attempt to make a seat from rushes until you have had a certain amount of practise with Hong Kong grass, but once you are familiar with the method and can follow it more or less automatically, you should be able to manage it quite successfully.

Stools covered by this method must always be worked with rounded rope-like material. Flat seating is quite unsuitable because you would be obliged to turn it at right angles at every corner and would thus be unable to make it lie flat.

Woven chair or stool seats made from narrow plastic or

leather strips are popular and are worked in much the same way as those of the woven grass, except that the warp and weft are both put on before the weaving is begun. Measure the width of your stool from the outside edge of one rail to the outside edge of the opposite one, plus about 3″ to allow for the weaving and to give you something to hold when you pull the strands tight. Nail the ends of one row of strips across the back of the frame, putting the edge of the strips level with the edge of the frame and using, according to their size and the width of the strips, one or two domed brass-headed nails of the type used by upholsterers. Make a similar row of strips on the right hand side. Weave the strap nearest to the back rail under and over the second row of strips, as close to the edge as possible. Fix in place for the time being with a drawing pin. Continue in this way until all the straps are in place, then remove the pins one by one, pull the straps tight and nail down. Trim off all the ends neatly.

If desired, the straps can be taken right round the rails and be nailed in place underneath, out of sight. This makes a much better job, but naturally takes more material. The extra amount needed must be calculated according to the thickness of the wood used for the rails.

Whatever method is used for making stool tops and chair seats and whatever material is put into them, you must always work as evenly as you possibly can, not only because even work looks better, but because it makes sure that each separate thread will take its fair share of the weight and so make the seat last longer.

CHAPTER X

Dyeing Reeds and Raffia: Vegetable dyes — soft suitable colours. A mordant needed to "fix" the dye — preparation and use. **Dyeing:** Making the dye bath — time required — the dyeing process. **Sources of colour:** Natural materials used by the American Indian — use of barks, roots, leaves, nuts — other sources.

MANY basket makers like to dye their own materials with natural vegetable products. Aniline dyes are frowned on for this purpose, as it is felt that the strong and sometimes garish colours they produce are not in keeping with the textures of reeds and raffia. Beautiful soft colours are obtained through the use of vegetable dyes.

If you are making baskets for profit, of course, you will probably prefer to buy your own materials already coloured and prepared, to save time and effort. If, however, you are pursuing basketry purely as a craft or hobby, you may enjoy experimenting with both the available dyes and those you can make yourself from local plants and tree barks.

Dyeing should be done in clear weather rather than on rainy days. Soft water is necessary. If local water contains a good deal of lime or other earthy substances, rain water is preferable. If using rain water is not feasible, you can neutralize the hard local water by adding acetic acid (vinegar).

To "fix" the dye your material will require a mordant. Alum, which is easy to come by, is a satisfactory mordant. About three ounces dissolved in a quart of water is generally the right proportion, though materials differ in their response to mordants and it may sometimes be necessary to experiment in order to find the correct proportion.

When the alum has dissolved completely, place the material to be dyed in the solution and leave it to soak for several hours—even overnight. This will allow the fibres of the reeds or raffia to take up the mordant, which assures that the dyes will be permanently fixed.

After your material has soaked in the mordant for several hours, immerse it in the dye bath while it is still damp. For dyeing, use containers only of brass, copper, enamel or porcelain. Do not use an iron vessel, which might ruin the colour.

To prepare the dye solution, dissolve the dye matter by boiling in an enamel container. A good average ratio is two ounces of dye powder to a gallon of water. If this produces too strong a colour, dilute it with more water. If the colour is not deep enough, add more dye stuff. This is the sort of procedure that is mastered through practice and experience. The length of time needed to arrive at the desired colour is also variable. Generally half an hour is enough. When the right colour is attained, strain the water to remove any sediment.

Now take the material you wish to dye, which has already soaked in the mordant solution as described, and place it in the boiling dye bath. Be sure it *is* boiling. The dyeing process, as has been said, may take about half an hour— sometimes longer, when a deep colour is wanted. During the dyeing process, turn the material over from time to time, using a wooden stick, to assure even colouring.

Sources of colour: The American Indians, of course, used the materials at hand to make their dye stuffs. Some of these, or similar natural products, may be available in your community. Others may be purchased through your local druggist. This procedure may take a little time, and your druggist will want you to buy at least a quarter of a pound of any one product to make it worth his while to put through a special order to his wholesaler or jobber. Prices fluctuate and availability on products of this type is uncertain, as some of them are imported from the Orient and the Middle East. Indigo is the least expensive, dragon's blood the most expensive, though not exorbitant—perhaps a dollar for a quarter of a pound or thereabouts.

Black: The Indians made their blacks from charcoal, from maidenhair fern stems or from the peeled pod of the martynia, which is jet black. Black can also be made from iris roots or young blackberry shoots.

Brown, tan and beige: The Indians obtained dark brown

from the extract of willow bark or alder bark. Brown dye can likewise be made from walnut or hickory nut shells, from butternut bark or from the bark of pine or maple trees. Walnut shells, gathered in the fall, should be soaked for several hours and then boiled for twenty minutes. (Walnut shells gathered in the spring, incidentally, and treated in the same way, will produce a soft green.) As you doubtless know, you can also make brown by boiling coffee or tea leaves. For a tan or beige boil them a shorter time. Sumac leaves and stems produce tan, while the fruit of the sumac gives a pink beige.

Reds: The Indians obtained their reds from the roots of the yucca and from wild berries. You may already at some time have made red dyes from red currants, cranberries or beets. These give a dull red. A purple-red may be made from poke berries. If you use these, take care not to get the dye on your hands, as it is hard to remove. Cochineal, an animal dye which gives a deep dark red, can be ordered through your druggist.

Yellow and orange: American saffron, which your druggist probably has in stock, produces a bright yellow. Spanish saffron, which gives a beautiful orange-yellow, may not be available but he may be able to get it for you. He will also be able to order dragon's blood, which gives a splendid orange. A dull yellow may be obtained from onion skins. An attractive yellow can easily be made from iron rust, by placing small pieces of rusted iron in a vessel of water. Other sources of yellow are pear, plum, poplar or privet leaves.

Purples: Purple can be obtained from the petals of the purple iris, a reddish purple from dandelion roots.

Green: Elder leaves and lily-of-the-valley leaves are among the sources of green.

Blues: Blues are made from indigo. This is tricky to use, as it dissolves only in sulphuric acid, which must be neutralized by adding soda before the materials to be dyed are immersed. Indigo, which is not recommended for the amateur dyer, may be ordered through your local druggist.

If you have had experience in mixing and blending colours, it will stand you in good stead when you begin to dye your own materials. Sometimes combining two or more dye stuffs will produce an unexpectedly beautiful colour. Be sure, however, when you are mixing your own colours, that you make a sufficient quantity to dye all the material for the article you are making. It may be difficult or impossible to reproduce a colour you have mixed.

If you have not had experience in the use of colour, a certain amount of trial and error will be needed. There may be information at your public library on the natural products of your locality that have been used successfully for dye making. Local teachers, craft workers and housewives of the older generation may also be able to give you useful suggestions on the subject. By whatever means you arrive at a knowledge of dyeing, you will find that this work can add immensely to the creative pleasure of the craft.

The mention of any product or supplier is offered purely to assist the reader, with the same informational and educational purpose as the reading list.

SUGGESTED READING — BOOKS

Begg, Annie.	RAFFIA (Pitman)
Brazer, Esther.	EARLY AMERICAN DECORATION (Pond-Ekberg)
Brinley, Rosemary.	RAFFIA WORK (Dover)
Chapman, Suzanne.	EARLY AMERICAN DESIGN MOTIFS (Dover)
Gallinger, O. and Benson, O.	HAND WEAVING WITH REEDS AND FIBERS (Pitman)
Hutchins, Mabel.	CREATIVE HANDICRAFTS (Sentinel)
Knock, A. G.	FINE WILLOW BASKETRY (Dryad)
Lee, Martha.	BASKETRY AND RELATED ARTS (Van Nostrand)
Parkhill, M. and Spaeth, D.	IT'S FUN TO MAKE THINGS (Barnes)
Reynolds, Harry.	LOW COST CRAFTS FOR EVERYONE (Blue Ribbon)
Walsh, Henry	THE MAKE-IT-YOURSELF BOOK OF HANDICRAFTS (Blakiston)

PERIODICALS

The magazines *Profitable Hobbies* and *Craft Horizons* occasionally run articles of interest to basketmakers. Some of the mail order firms dealing in craft supplies also issue booklets of instructions on basketry projects.

INDEX

A CATALOGUE OF
SELECTED DOVER BOOKS
IN ALL FIELDS OF INTEREST

A CATALOGUE OF SELECTED DOVER
BOOKS IN ALL FIELDS OF INTEREST

RACKHAM'S COLOR ILLUSTRATIONS FOR WAGNER'S RING. Rackham's finest mature work—all 64 full-color watercolors in a faithful and lush interpretation of the *Ring*. Full-sized plates on coated stock of the paintings used by opera companies for authentic staging of Wagner. Captions aid in following complete Ring cycle. Introduction. 64 illustrations plus vignettes. 72pp. 8⅝ x 11¼.   23779-6 Pa. $6.00

CONTEMPORARY POLISH POSTERS IN FULL COLOR, edited by Joseph Czestochowski. 46 full-color examples of brilliant school of Polish graphic design, selected from world's first museum (near Warsaw) dedicated to poster art. Posters on circuses, films, plays, concerts all show cosmopolitan influences, free imagination. Introduction. 48pp. 9⅜ x 12¼.
23780-X Pa. $6.00

GRAPHIC WORKS OF EDVARD MUNCH, Edvard Munch. 90 haunting, evocative prints by first major Expressionist artist and one of the greatest graphic artists of his time: *The Scream, Anxiety, Death Chamber, The Kiss, Madonna,* etc. Introduction by Alfred Werner. 90pp. 9 x 12.
23765-6 Pa. $5.00

THE GOLDEN AGE OF THE POSTER, Hayward and Blanche Cirker. 70 extraordinary posters in full colors, from Maitres de l'Affiche, Mucha, Lautrec, Bradley, Cheret, Beardsley, many others. Total of 78pp. 9⅜ x 12¼.   22753-7 Pa. $6.95

THE NOTEBOOKS OF LEONARDO DA VINCI, edited by J. P. Richter. Extracts from manuscripts reveal great genius; on painting, sculpture, anatomy, sciences, geography, etc. Both Italian and English. 186 ms. pages reproduced, plus 500 additional drawings, including studies for *Last Supper,* Sforza monument, etc. 860pp. 7⅞ x 10¾. (Available in U.S. only)
22572-0, 22573-9 Pa., Two-vol. set $19.90

THE CODEX NUTTALL, as first edited by Zelia Nuttall. Only inexpensive edition, in full color, of a pre-Columbian Mexican (Mixtec) book. 88 color plates show kings, gods, heroes, temples, sacrifices. New explanatory, historical introduction by Arthur G. Miller. 96pp. 11⅜ x 8½. (Available in U.S. only)   23168-2 Pa. $7.95

UNE SEMAINE DE BONTÉ, A SURREALISTIC NOVEL IN COLLAGE, Max Ernst. Masterpiece created out of 19th-century periodical illustrations, explores worlds of terror and surprise. Some consider this Ernst's greatest work. 208pp. 8⅛ x 11.   23252-2 Pa. $6.00

DRAWINGS OF WILLIAM BLAKE, William Blake. 92 plates from Book of Job, *Divine Comedy, Paradise Lost,* visionary heads, mythologic figures, Laocoon, etc. Selection, introduction, commentary by Sir Ge Keynes. 178pp. 8⅛ x 11.   22303-5 Pa

ENGRAVINGS OF HOGARTH, William Hogarth. 101 of Hog greatest works: *Rake's Progress, Harlot's Progress, Illustrations for Hudib Before and After, Beer Street and Gin Lane,* many more. Full commentar 256pp. 11 x 13¾.   22479-1 Pa. $12.95

DAUMIER: 120 GREAT LITHOGRAPHS, Honore Daumier. Wide-ranging collection of lithographs by the greatest caricaturist of the 19th century. Concentrates on eternally popular series on lawyers, on married life, on liberated women, etc. Selection, introduction, and notes on plates by Charles F. Ramus. Total of 158pp. 9⅜ x 12¼.   23512-2 Pa. $6.00

DRAWINGS OF MUCHA, Alphonse Maria Mucha. Work reveals drafts-man of highest caliber: studies for famous posters and paintings, render-ings for book illustrations and ads, etc. 70 works, 9 in color; including 6 items not drawings. Introduction. List of illustrations. 72pp. 9⅜ x 12¼. (Available in U.S. only)   23672-2 Pa. $4.50

GIOVANNI BATTISTA PIRANESI: DRAWINGS IN THE PIERPONT MORGAN LIBRARY, Giovanni Battista Piranesi. For first time ever all of Morgan Library's collection, world's largest. 167 illustrations of rare Piranesi drawings—archeological, architectural, decorative and visionary. Essay, detailed list of drawings, chronology, captions. Edited by Felice Stampfle. 144pp. 9⅜ x 12¼.   23714-1 Pa. $7.50

NEW YORK ETCHINGS (1905-1949), John Sloan. All of important American artist's N.Y. life etchings. 67 works include some of his best art; also lively historical record—Greenwich Village, tenement scenes. Edited by Sloan's widow. Introduction and captions. 79pp. 8⅜ x 11¼.
                                    23651-X Pa. $5.00

CHINESE PAINTING AND CALLIGRAPHY: A PICTORIAL SURVEY, Wan-go Weng. 69 fine examples from John M. Crawford's matchless private collection: landscapes, birds, flowers, human figures, etc., plus calligraphy. Every basic form included: hanging scrolls, handscrolls, album leaves, fans, etc. 109 illustrations. Introduction. Captions. 192pp. 8⅞ x 11¾.
                                    23707-9 Pa. $7.95

DRAWINGS OF REMBRANDT, edited by Seymour Slive. Updated Lipp-mann, Hofstede de Groot edition, with definitive scholarly apparatus. All portraits, biblical sketches, landscapes, nudes, Oriental figures, classical studies, together with selection of work by followers. 550 illustrations. Total of 630pp. 9⅛ x 12¼.   21485-0, 21486-9 Pa., Two-vol. set $17.90

THE DISASTERS OF WAR, Francisco Goya. 83 etchings record horrors of Napoleonic wars in Spain and war in general. Reprint of 1st edition, plus 3 additional plates. Introduction by Philip Hofer. 97pp. 9⅜ x 8¼.
                                    21872-4 Pa. $4.50

THE EARLY WORK OF AUBREY BEARDSLEY, Aubrey Beardsley. 157 plates, 2 in color: *Manon Lescaut, Madame Bovary, Morte Darthur, Salome,* other. Introduction by H. Marillier. 182pp. 8⅛ x 11. 21816-3 Pa. $6.50

THE LATER WORK OF AUBREY BEARDSLEY, Aubrey Beardsley. Exotic masterpieces of full maturity: *Venus and Tannhauser, Lysistrata, Rape of the Lock, Volpone,* Savoy material, etc. 174 plates, 2 in color. 186pp. 8⅛ x 11. 21817-1 Pa. $5.95

THOMAS NAST'S CHRISTMAS DRAWINGS, Thomas Nast. Almost all Christmas drawings by creator of image of Santa Claus as we know it, and one of America's foremost illustrators and political cartoonists. 66 illustrations. 3 illustrations in color on covers. 96pp. 8⅜ x 11¼.
23660-9 Pa. $3.50

THE DORÉ ILLUSTRATIONS FOR DANTE'S DIVINE COMEDY, Gustave Doré. All 135 plates from Inferno, Purgatory, Paradise; fantastic tortures, infernal landscapes, celestial wonders. Each plate with appropriate (translated) verses. 141pp. 9 x 12. 23231-X Pa. $5.00

DORÉ'S ILLUSTRATIONS FOR RABELAIS, Gustave Doré. 252 striking illustrations of *Gargantua and Pantagruel* books by foremost 19th-century illustrator. Including 60 plates, 192 delightful smaller illustrations. 153pp. 9 x 12. 23656-0 Pa. $6.00

LONDON: A PILGRIMAGE, Gustave Doré, Blanchard Jerrold. Squalor, riches, misery, beauty of mid-Victorian metropolis; 55 wonderful plates, 125 other illustrations, full social, cultural text by Jerrold. 191pp. of text. 9⅜ x 12¼. 22306-X Pa. $7.00

THE RIME OF THE ANCIENT MARINER, Gustave Doré, S. T. Coleridge. Dore's finest work, 34 plates capture moods, subtleties of poem. Full text. Introduction by Millicent Rose. 77pp. 9¼ x 12. 22305-1 Pa. $4.50

THE DORE BIBLE ILLUSTRATIONS, Gustave Doré. All wonderful, detailed plates: Adam and Eve, Flood, Babylon, Life of Jesus, etc. Brief King James text with each plate. Introduction by Millicent Rose. 241 plates. 241pp. 9 x 12. 23004-X Pa. $6.95

THE COMPLETE ENGRAVINGS, ETCHINGS AND DRYPOINTS OF ALBRECHT DURER. "Knight, Death and Devil"; "Melencolia," and more—all Dürer's known works in all three media, including 6 works formerly attributed to him. 120 plates. 235pp. 8⅜ x 11¼.
22851-7 Pa. $7.50

MECHANICK EXERCISES ON THE WHOLE ART OF PRINTING, Joseph Moxon. First complete book (1683-4) ever written about typography, a compendium of everything known about printing at the latter part of 17th century. Reprint of 2nd (1962) Oxford Univ. Press edition. 74 illustrations. Total of 550pp. 6⅛ x 9¼. 23617-X Pa. $7.95

THE COMPLETE WOODCUTS OF ALBRECHT DURER, edited by Dr. W. Kurth. 346 in all: "Old Testament," "St. Jerome," "Passion," "Life of Virgin," Apocalypse," many others. Introduction by Campbell Dodgson. 285pp. 8½ x 12¼. 21097-9 Pa. $7.50

DRAWINGS OF ALBRECHT DURER, edited by Heinrich Wolfflin. 81 plates show development from youth to full style. Many favorites; many new. Introduction by Alfred Werner. 96pp. 8⅛ x 11. 22352-3 Pa. $6.00

THE HUMAN FIGURE, Albrecht Dürer. Experiments in various techniques—stereometric, progressive proportional, and others. Also life studies that rank among finest ever done. Complete reprinting of *Dresden Sketchbook*. 170 plates. 355pp. 8⅜ x 11¼. 21042-1 Pa. $7.95

OF THE JUST SHAPING OF LETTERS, Albrecht Dürer. Renaissance artist explains design of Roman majuscules by geometry, also Gothic lower and capitals. Grolier Club edition. 43pp. 7⅞ x 10¾ 21306-4 Pa. $3.00

TEN BOOKS ON ARCHITECTURE, Vitruvius. The most important book ever written on architecture. Early Roman aesthetics, technology, classical orders, site selection, all other aspects. Stands behind everything since. Morgan translation. 331pp. 5⅜ x 8½. 20645-9 Pa. $5.00

THE FOUR BOOKS OF ARCHITECTURE, Andrea Palladio. 16th-century classic responsible for Palladian movement and style. Covers classical architectural remains, Renaissance revivals, classical orders, etc. 1738 Ware English edition. Introduction by A. Placzek. 216 plates. 110pp. of text. 9½ x 12¾. 21308-0 Pa. $10.00

HORIZONS, Norman Bel Geddes. Great industrialist stage designer, "father of streamlining," on application of aesthetics to transportation, amusement, architecture, etc. 1932 prophetic account; function, theory, specific projects. 222 illustrations. 312pp. 7⅞ x 10¾. 23514-9 Pa. $6.95

FRANK LLOYD WRIGHT'S FALLINGWATER, Donald Hoffmann. Full, illustrated story of conception and building of Wright's masterwork at Bear Run, Pa. 100 photographs of site, construction, and details of completed structure. 112pp. 9¼ x 10. 23671-4 Pa. $5.95

THE ELEMENTS OF DRAWING, John Ruskin. Timeless classic by great Viltorian; starts with basic ideas, works through more difficult. Many practical exercises. 48 illustrations. Introduction by Lawrence Campbell. 228pp. 5⅜ x 8½. 22730-8 Pa. $3.75

GIST OF ART, John Sloan. Greatest modern American teacher, Art Students League, offers innumerable hints, instructions, guided comments to help you in painting. Not a formal course. 46 illustrations. Introduction by Helen Sloan. 200pp. 5⅜ x 8½. 23435-5 Pa. $4.00

THE ANATOMY OF THE HORSE, George Stubbs. Often considered the great masterpiece of animal anatomy. Full reproduction of 1766 edition, plus prospectus; original text and modernized text. 36 plates. Introduction by Eleanor Garvey. 121pp. 11 x 14¾. 23402-9 Pa. $8.95

BRIDGMAN'S LIFE DRAWING, George B. Bridgman. More than 500 illustrative drawings and text teach you to abstract the body into its major masses, use light and shade, proportion; as well as specific areas of anatomy, of which Bridgman is master. 192pp. 6½ x 9¼. (Available in U.S. only) 22710-3 Pa. $4.50

ART NOUVEAU DESIGNS IN COLOR, Alphonse Mucha, Maurice Verneuil, Georges Auriol. Full-color reproduction of *Combinaisons ornementales* (c. 1900) by Art Nouveau masters. Floral, animal, geometric, interlacings, swashes—borders, frames, spots—all incredibly beautiful. 60 plates, hundreds of designs. 9⅜ x 8-1/16. 22885-1 Pa. $4.50

FULL-COLOR FLORAL DESIGNS IN THE ART NOUVEAU STYLE, E. A. Seguy. 166 motifs, on 40 plates, from *Les fleurs et leurs applications decoratives* (1902): borders, circular designs, repeats, allovers, "spots." All in authentic Art Nouveau colors. 48pp. 9⅜ x 12¼. 23439-8 Pa. $5.00

A DIDEROT PICTORIAL ENCYCLOPEDIA OF TRADES AND IN-DUSTRY, edited by Charles C. Gillispie. 485 most interesting plates from the great French Encyclopedia of the 18th century show hundreds of working figures, artifacts, process, land and cityscapes; glassmaking, papermaking, metal extraction, construction, weaving, making furniture, clothing, wigs, dozens of other activities. Plates fully explained. 920pp. 9 x 12. 22284-5, 22285-3 Clothbd., Two-vol. set $40.00

HANDBOOK OF EARLY ADVERTISING ART, Clarence P. Hornung. Largest collection of copyright-free early and antique advertising art ever compiled. Over 6,000 illustrations, from Franklin's time to the 1890's for special effects, novelty. Valuable source, almost inexhaustible.
Pictorial Volume. Agriculture, the zodiac, animals, autos, birds, Christmas, fire engines, flowers, trees, musical instruments, ships, games and sports, much more. Arranged by subject matter and use. 237 plates. 288pp. 9 x 12. 20122-8 Clothbd. $15.00

Typographical Volume. Roman and Gothic faces ranging from 10 point to 300 point, "Barnum," German and Old English faces, script, logotypes, scrolls and flourishes, 1115 ornamental initials, 67 complete alphabets, more. 310 plates. 320pp. 9 x 12. 20123-6 Clothbd. $15.00

CALLIGRAPHY (CALLIGRAPHIA LATINA), J. G. Schwandner. High point of 18th-century ornamental calligraphy. Very ornate initials, scrolls, borders, cherubs, birds, lettered examples. 172pp. 9 x 13. 20475-8 Pa. $7.95

CATALOGUE OF DOVER BOOKS

ART FORMS IN NATURE, Ernst Haeckel. Multitude of strangely beautiful natural forms: Radiolaria, Foraminifera, jellyfishes, fungi, turtles, bats, etc. All 100 plates of the 19th-century evolutionist's *Kunstformen der Natur* (1904). 100pp. 9⅜ x 12¼. 22987-4 Pa. $5.00

CHILDREN: A PICTORIAL ARCHIVE FROM NINETEENTH-CENTURY SOURCES, edited by Carol Belanger Grafton. 242 rare, copyright-free wood engravings for artists and designers. Widest such selection available. All illustrations in line. 119pp. 8⅜ x 11¼. 23694-3 Pa. $4.00

WOMEN: A PICTORIAL ARCHIVE FROM NINETEENTH-CENTURY SOURCES, edited by Jim Harter. 391 copyright-free wood engravings for artists and designers selected from rare periodicals. Most extensive such collection available. All illustrations in line. 128pp. 9 x 12. 23703-6 Pa. $4.95

ARABIC ART IN COLOR, Prisse d'Avennes. From the greatest ornamentalists of all time—50 plates in color, rarely seen outside the Near East, rich in suggestion and stimulus. Includes 4 plates on covers. 46pp. 9⅜ x 12¼. 23658-7 Pa. $6.00

AUTHENTIC ALGERIAN CARPET DESIGNS AND MOTIFS, edited by June Beveridge. Algerian carpets are world famous. Dozens of geometrical motifs are charted on grids, color-coded, for weavers, needleworkers, craftsmen, designers. 53 illustrations plus 4 in color. 48pp. 8¼ x 11. (Available in U.S. only) 23650-1 Pa. $1.75

DICTIONARY OF AMERICAN PORTRAITS, edited by Hayward and Blanche Cirker. 4000 important Americans, earliest times to 1905, mostly in clear line. Politicians, writers, soldiers, scientists, inventors, industrialists, Indians, Blacks, women, outlaws, etc. Identificatory information. 756pp. 9¼ x 12¾. 21823-6 Clothbd. $65.00

HOW THE OTHER HALF LIVES, Jacob A. Riis. Journalistic record of filth, degradation, upward drive in New York immigrant slums, shops, around 1900. New edition includes 100 original Riis photos, monuments of early photography. 233pp. 10 x 7⅞. 22012-5 Pa. $7.00

NEW YORK IN THE THIRTIES, Berenice Abbott. Noted photographer's fascinating study of city shows new buildings that have become famous and old sights that have disappeared forever. Insightful commentary. 97 photographs. 97pp. 11⅜ x 10. 22967-X Pa. $6.00

MEN AT WORK, Lewis W. Hine. Famous photographic studies of construction workers, railroad men, factory workers and coal miners. New supplement of 18 photos on Empire State building construction. New introduction by Jonathan L. Doherty. Total of 69 photos. 63pp. 8 x 10¾. 23475-4 Pa. $4.00

THE DEPRESSION YEARS AS PHOTOGRAPHED BY ARTHUR ROTH-STEIN, Arthur Rothstein. First collection devoted entirely to the work of outstanding 1930s photographer: famous dust storm photo, ragged children, unemployed, etc. 120 photographs. Captions. 119pp. 9¼ x 10¾.
23590-4 Pa. **$5.95**

CAMERA WORK: A PICTORIAL GUIDE, Alfred Stieglitz. All 559 illustrations and plates from the most important periodical in the history of art photography, Camera Work (1903-17). Presented four to a page, reduced in size but still clear, in strict chronological order, with complete captions. Three indexes. Glossary. Bibliography. 176pp. 8⅜ x 11¼.
23591-2 Pa. **$6.95**

ALVIN LANGDON COBURN, PHOTOGRAPHER, Alvin L. Coburn. Revealing autobiography by one of greatest photographers of 20th century gives insider's version of Photo-Secession, plus comments on his own work. 77 photographs by Coburn. Edited by Helmut and Alison Gernsheim. 160pp. 8⅛ x 11.
23685-4 Pa. **$6.00**

NEW YORK IN THE FORTIES, Andreas Feininger. 162 brilliant photographs by the well-known photographer, formerly with Life magazine, show commuters, shoppers, Times Square at night, Harlem nightclub, Lower East Side, etc. Introduction and full captions by John von Hartz. 181pp. 9¼ x 10¾.
23585-8 Pa. **$6.95**

GREAT NEWS PHOTOS AND THE STORIES BEHIND THEM, John Faber. Dramatic volume of 140 great news photos, 1855 through 1976, and revealing stories behind them, with both historical and technical information. Hindenburg disaster, shooting of Oswald, nomination of Jimmy Carter, etc. 160pp. 8¼ x 11.
23667-6 Pa. **$6.00**

THE ART OF THE CINEMATOGRAPHER, Leonard Maltin. Survey of American cinematography history and anecdotal interviews with 5 masters—Arthur Miller, Hal Mohr, Hal Rosson, Lucien Ballard, and Conrad Hall. Very large selection of behind-the-scenes production photos. 105 photographs. Filmographies. Index. Originally Behind the Camera. 144pp. 8¼ x 11.
23686-2 Pa. **$5.00**

DESIGNS FOR THE THREE-CORNERED HAT (LE TRICORNE), Pablo Picasso. 32 fabulously rare drawings—including 31 color illustrations of costumes and accessories—for 1919 production of famous ballet. Edited by Parmenia Migel, who has written new introduction. 48pp. 9⅜ x 12¼. (Available in U.S. only)
23709-5 Pa. **$5.00**

NOTES OF A FILM DIRECTOR, Sergei Eisenstein. Greatest Russian filmmaker explains montage, making of Alexander Nevsky, aesthetics; comments on self, associates, great rivals (Chaplin), similar material. 78 illustrations. 240pp. 5⅜ x 8½.
22392-2 Pa. **$7.00**

HOLLYWOOD GLAMOUR PORTRAITS, edited by John Kobal. 145 photos capture the stars from 1926-49, the high point in portrait photography. Gable, Harlow, Bogart, Bacall, Hedy Lamarr, Marlene Dietrich, Robert Montgomery, Marlon Brando, Veronica Lake; 94 stars in all. Full background on photographers, technical aspects, much more. Total of 160pp. 8⅜ x 11¼. 23352-9 Pa. $6.95

THE NEW YORK STAGE: FAMOUS PRODUCTIONS IN PHOTO-GRAPHS, edited by Stanley Appelbaum. 148 photographs from Museum of City of New York show 142 plays, 1883-1939. *Peter Pan, The Front Page, Dead End, Our Town,* O'Neill, hundreds of actors and actresses, etc. Full indexes. 154pp. 9½ x 10. 23241-7 Pa. $6.00

DIALOGUES CONCERNING TWO NEW SCIENCES, Galileo Galilei. Encompassing 30 years of experiment and thought, these dialogues deal with geometric demonstrations of fracture of solid bodies, cohesion, leverage, speed of light and sound, pendulums, falling bodies, accelerated motion, etc. 300pp. 5⅜ x 8½. 60099-8 Pa. $5.50

THE GREAT OPERA STARS IN HISTORIC PHOTOGRAPHS, edited by James Camner. 343 portraits from the 1850s to the 1940s: Tamburini, Mario, Caliapin, Jeritza, Melchior, Melba, Patti, Pinza, Schipa, Caruso, Farrar, Steber, Gobbi, and many more—270 performers in all. Index. 199pp. 8⅜ x 11¼. 23575-0 Pa. $7.50

J. S. BACH, Albert Schweitzer. Great full-length study of Bach, life, background to music, music, by foremost modern scholar. Ernest Newman translation. 650 musical examples. Total of 928pp. 5⅜ x 8½. (Available in U.S. only) 21631-4, 21632-2 Pa., Two-vol. set $12.00

COMPLETE PIANO SONATAS, Ludwig van Beethoven. All sonatas in the fine Schenker edition, with fingering, analytical material. One of best modern editions. Total of 615pp. 9 x 12. (Available in U.S. only) 23134-8, 23135-6 Pa., Two-vol. set $17.90

KEYBOARD MUSIC, J. S. Bach. Bach-Gesellschaft edition. For harpsichord, piano, other keyboard instruments. English Suites, French Suites, Six Partitas, Goldberg Variations, Two-Part Inventions, Three-Part Sinfonias. 312pp. 8⅛ x 11. (Available in U.S. only) 22360-4 Pa. $7.95

FOUR SYMPHONIES IN FULL SCORE, Franz Schubert. Schubert's four most popular symphonies: No. 4 in C Minor ("Tragic"); No. 5 in B-flat Major; No. 8 in B Minor ("Unfinished"); No. 9 in C Major ("Great"). Breitkopf & Hartel edition. Study score. 261pp. 9⅜ x 12¼. 23681-1 Pa. $8.95

THE AUTHENTIC GILBERT & SULLIVAN SONGBOOK, W. S. Gilbert, A. S. Sullivan. Largest selection available; 92 songs, uncut, original keys, in piano rendering approved by Sullivan. Favorites and lesser-known fine numbers. Edited with plot synopses by James Spero. 3 illustrations. 399pp. 9 x 12. 23482-7 Pa.$10.95

PRINCIPLES OF ORCHESTRATION, Nikolay Rimsky-Korsakov. Great classical orchestrator provides fundamentals of tonal resonance, progression of parts, voice and orchestra, tutti effects, much else in major document. 330pp. of musical excerpts. 489pp. 6½ x 9¼. 21266-1 Pa. $7.50

TRISTAN UND ISOLDE, Richard Wagner. Full orchestral score with complete instrumentation. Do not confuse with piano reduction. Commentary by Felix Mottl, great Wagnerian conductor and scholar. Study score. 655pp. 8⅛ x 11. 22915-7 Pa. $13.95

REQUIEM IN FULL SCORE, Giuseppe Verdi. Immensely popular with choral groups and music lovers. Republication of edition published by C. F. Peters, Leipzig, n. d. German frontmaker in English translation. Glossary. Text in Latin. Study score. 204pp. 9⅜ x 12¼. 23682-X Pa. $6.50

COMPLETE CHAMBER MUSIC FOR STRINGS, Felix Mendelssohn. All of Mendelssohn's chamber music: Octet, 2 Quintets, 6 Quartets, and Four Pieces for String Quartet. (Nothing with piano is included). Complete works edition (1874-7). Study score. 283 pp. 9⅜ x 12¼. 23679-X Pa. $7.50

POPULAR SONGS OF NINETEENTH-CENTURY AMERICA, edited by Richard Jackson. 64 most important songs: "Old Oaken Bucket," "Arkansas Traveler," "Yellow Rose of Texas," etc. Authentic original sheet music, full introduction and commentaries. 290pp. 9 x 12. 23270-0 Pa. $7.95

COLLECTED PIANO WORKS, Scott Joplin. Edited by Vera Brodsky Lawrence. Practically all of Joplin's piano works—rags, two-steps, marches, waltzes, etc., 51 works in all. Extensive introduction by Rudi Blesh. Total of 345pp. 9 x 12. 23106-2 Pa. $15.95

BASIC PRINCIPLES OF CLASSICAL BALLET, Agrippina Vaganova. Great Russian theoretician, teacher explains methods for teaching classical ballet; incorporates best from French, Italian, Russian schools. 118 illustrations. 175pp. 5⅜ x 8½. 22036-2 Pa. $2.75

CHINESE CHARACTERS, L. Wieger. Rich analysis of 2300 characters according to traditional systems into primitives. Historical-semantic analysis to phonetics (Classical Mandarin) and radicals. 820pp. 6⅛ x 9¼. 21321-8 Pa. $12.50

THE WARES OF THE MING DYNASTY, R. L. Hobson. Foremost scholar examines and illustrates many varieties of Ming (1368-1644). Famous blue and white, polychrome, lesser-known styles and shapes. 117 illustrations, 9 full color, of outstanding pieces. Total of 263pp. 6⅛ x 9¼. (Available in U.S. only) 23652-8 Pa. $6.00

AN ETYMOLOGICAL DICTIONARY OF MODERN ENGLISH, Ernest Weekley. Richest, fullest work, by foremost British lexicographer. Detailed word histories. Inexhaustible. Do not confuse this with *Concise Etymological Dictionary*, which is abridged. Total of 856pp. 6½ x 9¼. 21873-2, 21874-0 Pa., Two-vol. set $13.00

A MAYA GRAMMAR, Alfred M. Tozzer. Practical, useful English-language grammar by the Harvard anthropologist who was one of the three greatest American scholars in the area of Maya culture. Phonetics, grammatical processes, syntax, more. 301pp. 5⅜ x 8½. 23465-7 Pa. $4.00

THE JOURNAL OF HENRY D. THOREAU, edited by Bradford Torrey, F. H. Allen. Complete reprinting of 14 volumes, 1837-61, over two million words; the sourcebooks for *Walden*, etc. Definitive. All original sketches, plus 75 photographs. Introduction by Walter Harding. Total of 1804pp. 8½ x 12¼. 20312-3, 20313-1 Clothbd., Two-vol. set $80.00

CLASSIC GHOST STORIES, Charles Dickens and others. 18 wonderful stories you've wanted to reread: "The Monkey's Paw," "The House and the Brain," "The Upper Berth," "The Signalman," "Dracula's Guest," "The Tapestried Chamber," etc. Dickens, Scott, Mary Shelley, Stoker, etc. 330pp. 5⅜ x 8½. 20735-8 Pa. $4.50

SEVEN SCIENCE FICTION NOVELS, H. G. Wells. Full novels. *First Men in the Moon, Island of Dr. Moreau, War of the Worlds, Food of the Gods, Invisible Man, Time Machine, In the Days of the Comet.* A basic science-fiction library. 1015pp. 5⅜ x 8½. (Available in U.S. only) 20264-X Clothbd.$15.00

ARMADALE, Wilkie Collins. Third great mystery novel by the author of *The Woman in White* and *The Moonstone*. Ingeniously plotted narrative shows an exceptional command of character, incident and mood. Original magazine version with 40 illustrations. 597pp. 5⅜ x 8½. 23429-0 Pa. $7.95

FLATLAND, E. A. Abbott. Science-fiction classic explores life of 2-D being in 3-D world. Read also as introduction to thought about hyperspace. Introduction by Banesh Hoffmann. 16 illustrations. 103pp. 5⅜ x 8½. 20001-9 Pa. $2.75

AYESHA: THE RETURN OF "SHE," H. Rider Haggard. Virtuoso sequel featuring the great mythic creation, Ayesha, in an adventure that is fully as good as the first book, *She*. Original magazine version, with 47 original illustrations by Maurice Greiffenhagen. 189pp. 6½ x 9¼. 23649-8 Pa. $3.50

ORIENTAL RUGS, ANTIQUE AND MODERN, Walter A. Hawley. Persia, Turkey, Caucasus, Central Asia, China, other traditions. Best general survey of all aspects: styles and periods, manufacture, uses, symbols and their interpretation, and identification. 96 illustrations, 11 in color. 320pp. 6⅛ x 9¼. 22366-3 Pa. $6.95

CHINESE POTTERY AND PORCELAIN, R. L. Hobson. Detailed descriptions and analyses by former Keeper of the Department of Oriental Antiquities and Ethnography at the British Museum. Covers hundreds of pieces from primitive times to 1915. Still the standard text for most periods. 136 plates, 40 in full color. Total of 750pp. 5⅜ x 8½. 23253-0 Pa. $10.00

UNCLE SILAS, J. Sheridan LeFanu. Victorian Gothic mystery novel, considered by many best of period, even better than Collins or Dickens. Wonderful psychological terror. Introduction by Frederick Shroyer. 436pp. 5⅜ x 8½. 21715-9 Pa. **$6.95**

JURGEN, James Branch Cabell. The great erotic fantasy of the 1920's that delighted thousands, shocked thousands more. Full final text, Lane edition with 13 plates by Frank Pape. 346pp. 5⅜ x 8½.
23507-6 Pa. $4.50

THE CLAVERINGS, Anthony Trollope. Major novel, chronicling aspects of British Victorian society, personalities. Reprint of Cornhill serialization, 16 plates by M. Edwards; first reprint of full text. Introduction by Norman Donaldson. 412pp. 5⅜ x 8½. 23464-9 Pa. $5.00

KEPT IN THE DARK, Anthony Trollope. Unusual short novel about Victorian morality and abnormal psychology by the great English author. Probably the first American publication. Frontispiece by Sir John Millais. 92pp. 6½ x 9¼. 23609-9 Pa. $2.50

RALPH THE HEIR, Anthony Trollope. Forgotten tale of illegitimacy, inheritance. Master novel of Trollope's later years. Victorian country estates, clubs, Parliament, fox hunting, world of fully realized characters. Reprint of 1871 edition. 12 illustrations by F. A. Faser. 434pp. of text. 5⅜ x 8½. 23642-0 Pa. **$6.50**

YEKL and THE IMPORTED BRIDEGROOM AND OTHER STORIES OF THE NEW YORK GHETTO, Abraham Cahan. Film *Hester Street* based on *Yekl* (1896). Novel, other stories among first about Jewish immigrants of N.Y.'s East Side. Highly praised by W. D. Howells—Cahan "a new star of realism." New introduction by Bernard G. Richards. 240pp. 5⅜ x 8½. 22427-9 Pa. $3.50

THE HIGH PLACE, James Branch Cabell. Great fantasy writer's enchanting comedy of disenchantment set in 18th-century France. Considered by some critics to be even better than his famous *Jurgen*. 10 illustrations and numerous vignettes by noted fantasy artist Frank C. Pape. 320pp. 5⅜ x 8½. 23670-6 Pa. $4.00

ALICE'S ADVENTURES UNDER GROUND, Lewis Carroll. Facsimile of ms. Carroll gave Alice Liddell in 1864. Different in many ways from final Alice. Handlettered, illustrated by Carroll. Introduction by Martin Gardner. 128pp. 5⅜ x 8½. 21482-6 Pa. $2.50

FAVORITE ANDREW LANG FAIRY TALE BOOKS IN MANY COLORS, Andrew Lang. The four Lang favorites in a boxed set—the complete *Red, Green, Yellow* and *Blue* Fairy Books. 164 stories; 439 illustrations by Lancelot Speed, Henry Ford and G. P. Jacomb Hood. Total of about 1500pp. 5⅜ x 8½. 23407-X Boxed set, Pa. **$16.95**

HOUSEHOLD STORIES BY THE BROTHERS GRIMM. All the great Grimm stories: "Rumpelstiltskin," "Snow White," "Hansel and Gretel," etc., with 114 illustrations by Walter Crane. 269pp. 5⅜ x 8½.
21080-4 Pa. $3.50

SLEEPING BEAUTY, illustrated by Arthur Rackham. Perhaps the fullest, most delightful version ever, told by C. S. Evans. Rackham's best work. 49 illustrations. 110pp. 7⅞ x 10¾.
22756-1 Pa. $2.95

AMERICAN FAIRY TALES, L. Frank Baum. Young cowboy lassoes Father Time; dummy in Mr. Floman's department store window comes to life; and 10 other fairy tales. 41 illustrations by N. P. Hall, Harry Kennedy, Ike Morgan, and Ralph Gardner. 209pp. 5⅜ x 8½.
23643-9 Pa. $3.00

THE WONDERFUL WIZARD OF OZ, L. Frank Baum. Facsimile in full color of America's finest children's classic. Introduction by Martin Gardner. 143 illustrations by W. W. Denslow. 267pp. 5⅜ x 8½.
20691-2 Pa. $4.50

THE TALE OF PETER RABBIT, Beatrix Potter. The inimitable Peter's terrifying adventure in Mr. McGregor's garden, with all 27 wonderful, full-color Potter illustrations. 55pp. 4¼ x 5½. (Available in U.S. only)
22827-4 Pa. $1.50

THE STORY OF KING ARTHUR AND HIS KNIGHTS, Howard Pyle. Finest children's version of life of King Arthur. 48 illustrations by Pyle. 131pp. 6⅛ x 9¼.
21445-1 Pa. $5.95

CARUSO'S CARICATURES, Enrico Caruso. Great tenor's remarkable caricatures of self, fellow musicians, composers, others. Toscanini, Puccini, Farrar, etc. Impish, cutting, insightful. 473 illustrations. Preface by M. Sisca. 217pp. 8⅜ x 11¼.
23528-9 Pa. $6.95

PERSONAL NARRATIVE OF A PILGRIMAGE TO ALMADINAH AND MECCAH, Richard Burton. Great travel classic by remarkably colorful personality. Burton, disguised as a Moroccan, visited sacred shrines of Islam, narrowly escaping death. Wonderful observations of Islamic life, customs, personalities. 47 illustrations. Total of 959pp. 5⅜ x 8½.
21217-3, 21218-1 Pa., Two-vol. set $14.00

INCIDENTS OF TRAVEL IN YUCATAN, John L. Stephens. Classic (1843) exploration of jungles of Yucatan, looking for evidences of Maya civilization. Travel adventures, Mexican and Indian culture, etc. Total of 669pp. 5⅜ x 8½.
20926-1, 20927-X Pa., Two-vol. set $7.90

AMERICAN LITERARY AUTOGRAPHS FROM WASHINGTON IRVING TO HENRY JAMES, Herbert Cahoon, et al. Letters, poems, manuscripts of Hawthorne, Thoreau, Twain, Alcott, Whitman, 67 other prominent American authors. Reproductions, full transcripts and commentary. Plus checklist of all American Literary Autographs in The Pierpont Morgan Library. Printed on exceptionally high-quality paper. 136 illustrations. 212pp. 9⅛ x 12¼.
23548-3 Pa. $12.50

AN AUTOBIOGRAPHY, Margaret Sanger. Exciting personal account of hard-fought battle for woman's right to birth control, against prejudice, church, law. Foremost feminist document. 504pp. 5⅜ x 8½.

20470-7 Pa. $7.50

MY BONDAGE AND MY FREEDOM, Frederick Douglass. Born as a slave, Douglass became outspoken force in antislavery movement. The best of Douglass's autobiographies. Graphic description of slave life. Introduction by P. Foner. 464pp. 5⅜ x 8½.   22457-0 Pa. $6.50

LIVING MY LIFE, Emma Goldman. Candid, no holds barred account by foremost American anarchist: her own life, anarchist movement, famous contemporaries, ideas and their impact. Struggles and confrontations in America, plus deportation to U.S.S.R. Shocking inside account of persecution of anarchists under Lenin. 13 plates. Total of 944pp. 5⅜ x 8½.

22543-7, 22544-5 Pa., Two-vol. set $12.00

LETTERS AND NOTES ON THE MANNERS, CUSTOMS AND CONDITIONS OF THE NORTH AMERICAN INDIANS, George Catlin. Classic account of life among Plains Indians: ceremonies, hunt, warfare, etc. Dover edition reproduces for first time all original paintings. 312 plates. 572pp. of text. 6⅛ x 9¼.   22118-0, 22119-9 Pa.. Two-vol. set $12.00

THE MAYA AND THEIR NEIGHBORS, edited by Clarence L. Hay, others. Synoptic view of Maya civilization in broadest sense, together with Northern, Southern neighbors. Integrates much background, valuable detail not elsewhere. Prepared by greatest scholars: Kroeber, Morley, Thompson, Spinden, Vaillant, many others. Sometimes called Tozzer Memorial Volume. 60 illustrations, linguistic map. 634pp. 5⅜ x 8½.

23510-6 Pa. $10.00

HANDBOOK OF THE INDIANS OF CALIFORNIA, A. L. Kroeber. Foremost American anthropologist offers complete ethnographic study of each group. Monumental classic. 459 illustrations, maps. 995pp. 5⅜ x 8½.

23368-5 Pa. $13.00

SHAKTI AND SHAKTA, Arthur Avalon. First book to give clear, cohesive analysis of Shakta doctrine, Shakta ritual and Kundalini Shakti (yoga). Important work by one of world's foremost students of Shaktic and Tantric thought. 732pp. 5⅜ x 8½. (Available in U.S. only)

23645-5 Pa. $7.95

AN INTRODUCTION TO THE STUDY OF THE MAYA HIEROGLYPHS, Syvanus Griswold Morley. Classic study by one of the truly great figures in hieroglyph research. Still the best introduction for the student for reading Maya hieroglyphs. New introduction by J. Eric S. Thompson. 117 illustrations. 284pp. 5⅜ x 8½.   23108-9 Pa. $4.00

A STUDY OF MAYA ART, Herbert J. Spinden. Landmark classic interprets Maya symbolism, estimates styles, covers ceramics, architecture, murals, stone carvings as artforms. Still a basic book in area. New introduction by J. Eric Thompson. Over 750 illustrations. 341pp. 8⅜ x 11¼.

21235-1 Pa. $6.95

GEOMETRY, RELATIVITY AND THE FOURTH DIMENSION, Rudolf Rucker. Exposition of fourth dimension, means of visualization, concepts of relativity as Flatland characters continue adventures. Popular, easily followed yet accurate, profound. 141 illustrations. 133pp. 5⅜ x 8½.
23400-2 Pa. $2.75

THE ORIGIN OF LIFE, A. I. Oparin. Modern classic in biochemistry, the first rigorous examination of possible evolution of life from nitrocarbon compounds. Non-technical, easily followed. Total of 295pp. 5⅜ x 8½.
60213-3 Pa. $5.95

PLANETS, STARS AND GALAXIES, A. E. Fanning. Comprehensive introductory survey: the sun, solar system, stars, galaxies, universe, cosmology; quasars, radio stars, etc. 24pp. of photographs. 189pp. 5⅜ x 8½. (Available in U.S. only)
21680-2 Pa. $3.75

THE THIRTEEN BOOKS OF EUCLID'S ELEMENTS, translated with introduction and commentary by Sir Thomas L. Heath. Definitive edition. Textual and linguistic notes, mathematical analysis, 2500 years of critical commentary. Do not confuse with abridged school editions. Total of 1414pp. 5⅜ x 8½.   60088-2, 60089-0, 60090-4 Pa., Three-vol. set $19.50

Prices subject to change without notice.

Available at your book dealer or write for free catalogue to Dept. GI, Dover Publications, Inc., 180 Varick St., N.Y., N.Y. 10014. Dover publishes more than 175 books each year on science, elementary and advanced mathematics, biology, music, art, literary history, social sciences and other areas.